Maine Coon Cats as Pets

A Complete Maine Coon Cat Owner Guide

Maine Coon Cat Breeding, Where to Buy, Types, Care, Temperament, Cost, Health, Showing, Grooming, Diet and Much More Included!

By Lolly Brown

Foreword

Simply put, the Maine Coon Cat is a big cat - in its size as well as its heart. But despite their size, they are relatively low-maintenance pets that require no special attention or needs. They will usually attach to one particular person, and to this person they will show a kind of dog-like devotion, loyalty and affection. They are aptly named gentle giants - for Maine Coons are certainly a gentle bunch. They are usually not prone to rowdy behavior, and you'll probably be surprised to hear this oversized furball trilling instead of meowing!

Throughout the years, this affectionate but gorgeous breed has won its way into people's hearts and even onto the top ranks of America's show cats. They can thrive as mousers, as indoor cats, family pets, or show cats - yes, Maine Coons are as laid-back as they are pretty much adaptable wherever they live. Anything goes, this cat seems to say with a delightful yawn.

If you have been considering adding a Maine Coon to your household, read on. We will provide you with many of the pertinent information you might need or simply be curious about as you look into the possibility of bringing your own Maine Coon home.

Table of Contents

Introduction

What makes the difference between our cute domestic cats and the cats of the jungle? You might think it was their size, but you're probably going to change your mind once you see a Maine Coon cat.

Widely touted as the "giants of the cat world," Maine Coons are a large breed of cat - the first natural breed to emerge in the United States, and is now the official cat of its namesake - the state of Maine.

Maine Coons are among the most popular breed of cats today - recently ranked third in popularity among registered breeds, and they are making an absolute killing in the cat show circuit.

Not only are they popular show cats, they are also popular family cats, as they get along well with kids, with a large family, and even with other pets. Despite their large size, they can thrive well even as an indoor cat - and compared with some of the more exotic breeds, they are fairly low-maintenance. A weekly brushing is all that is required, and you can keep them looking downright decent.

Each cat comes with its own unique quirks and traits, but as a breed, Maine Coons have an even temperament, and provided proper socialization as kittens, they are loving, amiable, intelligent, affectionate, devoted, and goofy cats to have around. They are also pretty adaptable, and even a cat with the makings of a gorgeous show cat will not be above chasing a mouse once they are allowed into a natural environment. They are a hardy but good-looking breed, and while they will not be demanding of your attention, they will expect not to be ignored.

Maine Coons have a unique collection of various chirps and trills in addition to a cat's usual repertoire of meowing and yowling, and this can add pleasantly to the unique mix of traits that make the Maine Coon a distinctive and lovable breed.

If you have your heart set on adding a Maine Coon to your family, make sure you can provide him with the proper environment in which he can thrive. Within this book, you can learn more about this breed - from theories regarding its origins, the costs of keeping a Maine Coon, health and nutrition, training, grooming, and even breeding. Read on, and learn more about this wonderful breed of all-around American cat.

Glossary of Cat Terms

Abundism – Referring to a cat that has markings more prolific than is normal.

Acariasis – A type of mite infection.

ACF – Australian Cat Federation

Affix – A cattery name that follows the cat's registered name; cattery owner, not the breeder of the cat.

Agouti – A type of natural coloring pattern in which individual hairs have bands of light and dark coloring.

Ailurophile – A person who loves cats.

Albino – A type of genetic mutation which results in little to no pigmentation, in the eyes, skin, and coat.

Allbreed – Referring to a show that accepts all breeds or a judge who is qualified to judge all breeds.

Alley Cat – A non-pedigreed cat.

Alter – A desexed cat; a male cat that has been neutered or a female that has been spayed.

Amino Acid – The building blocks of protein; there are 22 types for cats, 11 of which can be synthesized and 11 which must come from the diet (see essential amino acid).

Anestrus – The period between estrus cycles in a female cat.

Any Other Variety (AOV) – A registered cat that doesn't conform to the breed standard.

ASH – American Shorthair, a breed of cat.

Back Cross – A type of breeding in which the offspring is mated back to the parent.

Balance – Referring to the cat's structure; proportional in accordance with the breed standard.

Barring – Describing the tabby's striped markings.

Base Color – The color of the coat.

Bicolor – A cat with patched color and white.

Blaze – A white coloring on the face, usually in the shape of an inverted V.

Bloodline – The pedigree of the cat.

Brindle – A type of coloring, a brownish or tawny coat with streaks of another color.

Castration – The surgical removal of a male cat's testicles.

Cat Show – An event where cats are shown and judged.

Cattery – A registered cat breeder; also, a place where cats may be boarded.

CFA – The Cat Fanciers Association.

Cobby – A compact body type.

Colony – A group of cats living wild outside.

Color Point – A type of coat pattern that is controlled by color point alleles; pigmentation on the tail, legs, face, and ears with an ivory or white coat.

Colostrum – The first milk produced by a lactating female; contains vital nutrients and antibodies.

Conformation – The degree to which a pedigreed cat adheres to the breed standard.

Cross Breed – The offspring produced by mating two distinct breeds.

Dam – The female parent.

Declawing – The surgical removal of the cat's claw and first toe joint.

Developed Breed – A breed that was developed through selective breeding and crossing with established breeds.

Down Hairs – The short, fine hairs closest to the body which keep the cat warm.

DSH – Domestic Shorthair.

Estrus – The reproductive cycle in female cats during which she becomes fertile and receptive to mating.

Fading Kitten Syndrome – Kittens that die within the first two weeks after birth; the cause is generally unknown.

Feral – A wild, untamed cat of domestic descent.

Gestation – Pregnancy; the period during which the fetuses develop in the female's uterus.

Guard Hairs – Coarse, outer hairs on the coat.

Harlequin – A type of coloring in which there are van markings of any color with the addition of small patches of the same color on the legs and body.

Inbreeding – The breeding of related cats within a closed group or breed.

Kibble – Another name for dry cat food.

Lilac – A type of coat color that is pale pinkish-gray.

Line – The pedigree of ancestors; family tree.

Litter – The name given to a group of kittens born at the same time from a single female.

Mask – A type of coloring seen on the face in some breeds.

Matts – Knots or tangles in the cat's fur.

Mittens – White markings on the feet of a cat.

Moggie – Another name for a mixed breed cat.

Mutation – A change in the DNA of a cell.

Mutation Breed – A breed of cat that resulted from a spontaneous mutation; ex: Cornish Rex and Sphynx.

Muzzle – The nose and jaws of an animal.

Natural Breed – A breed that developed without selective breeding or the assistance of humans.

Neutering – Desexing a male cat.

Open Show – A show in which spectators are allowed to view the judging.

Pads – The thick skin on the bottom of the feet.

Particolor – A type of coloration in which there are markings of two or more distinct colors.

Patched – A type of coloration in which there is any solid color, tabby, or tortoiseshell color plus white.

Pedigree – A purebred cat; the cat's papers showing its family history.

Pet Quality – A cat that is not deemed of high enough standard to be shown or bred.

Piebald – A cat with white patches of fur.

Points – Also color points; markings of contrasting color on the face, ears, legs, and tail.

Pricked – Referring to ears that sit upright.

Purebred – A pedigreed cat.

Queen – An intact female cat.

Roman Nose – A type of nose shape with a bump or arch.

Scruff – The loose skin on the back of a cat's neck.

Selective Breeding – A method of modifying or improving a breed by choosing cats with desirable traits.

Senior – A cat that is more than 5 but less than 7 years old.

Sire – The male parent of a cat.

Solid – Also self; a cat with a single coat color.

Spay – Desexing a female cat.

Stud – An intact male cat.

Tabby – A type of coat pattern consisting of a contrasting color over a ground color.

Tom Cat – An intact male cat.

Tortoiseshell – A type of coat pattern consisting of a mosaic of red or cream and another base color.

Tri-Color – A type of coat pattern consisting of three distinct colors in the coat.

Tuxedo – A black and white cat.

Unaltered – A cat that has not been desexed.

Chapter One: Understanding Maine Coon Cats

It seems that everybody loves Maine Coon cats. These big, lovable giants of the cat world are the first natural breed to emerge from the regions of northern America, and while their origins are shrouded in mystery, nobody has any doubts as to the gentleness, affection, and loyalty of these big cats.

Facts About Maine Coon Cats

Perhaps it was their size that inevitably brought them to the notice of humans, but they have lived alongside humans since the breed first began to make their appearance, serving first as mousers and then later on claiming the title of America's first show cat. This is a breed that emerged naturally from the influx and mixture of settlers and the local population during the European settlement of the East Coast. There was no human intervention during the creation of the breed, and the original Maine Coons were hardened by the harsh New England climate.

They are known for their long and furry coats with silky and flowing hair below the chin, on their bellies, and gracing their long and strong tails. This is a hardy breed, natural hunters, and have a distinctive calm and gentle temperament. Though they also have a goofy or comic side to their natures - which for some reason they never seem to outgrow. They do enjoy playtime!

Maine Coons come in all colors and coat patterns, but they are certainly known for their long, silky fur, their lynx-like ears, and their bushy tails that, when ringed, certainly looks much like a raccoon's tail! This is, in fact, the background for their name: Coon, short for Raccoon, appended to Maine, the state in which they emerged, and are now acknowleged to be the state cat.

Maine Coons are delightful cats, and they are a good pet choice even for first time owners. Despite their large size, they really do not require much save from the occasional playtime and displays of affection. They can thrive even as indoor cats, provided they are given sufficient running room, ample living furniture (pet beds, cat litters, scratching posts and toys), and enough attention.

They are variously nicknamed as "gentle giants" and the "dogs of the cat world" - and they do seem to exhibit both the gentleness that belies their giant stature, and dog-like qualities such as loyalty, devotion, attachment to their owners, and even a penchant for learning tricks. Maine Coons are intelligent, hardy creatures, and they are natural show cats who can flaunt their dignified beauty amidst a show hall. You might not think it - but that tiny kitten you just brought home will grow, and will keep growing, right into your hearts.

Summary of Maine Coon Cat Facts

Pedigree: unknown

Breed Size: medium to large

Weight: average 8 to 18 lbs (3.6 to 8.2 kg.)

Body Type: large body, robust bone structure, well-muscled

Coat Length: uneven coat length; shrt on the head and shoulders, gradually increasing in length along the back and sides, ending in full britches, long, shaggy belly fur, and full, long and flowing fur along the tail.

Coat Texture: soft but with body, falling smoothly and lies close to the body

Color: wide variety of colors with patterns ranging from solid, parti-colors, bi-colors, tabbies, shaded, and ticked

Eyes: eyes are large, with a slight oblique setting

Ears: large, wide at the base, moderately pointed and well-tufted

Tail: long, wide at the base and tapering, with full, long and flowing fur

Temperament: friendly, affectionate, loving, loyal and goofy

Strangers: cautious with strangers, though never mean or shy

Children: kind, playful, and very good with children

Other Pets: gets along with dogs and most other pets

Exercise Needs: provide adequate exercise and mental stimulation, such as perches, adequate running room, and sufficient playtime

Health Conditions: generally healthy but prone to some hereditary conditions such as Feline Hypertrophic Cardiomyopathy (HCM), Spinal Muscular Atrophy (SMA), Hip Dysplasia (HD), and Polycystic Kidney Disease (PKD)

Lifespan: average 9 to 13 years

Maine Coon Cat Breed History

Maine Coon cats are one of the oldest natural breeds in North America, and they are the first long-haired cat breed to emerge naturally from the USA. Being a natural breed, no human intervention was involved in their breeding, and so nobody really knows which strains were mixed to produce this very distinct feline.

All that we really have about their origins is speculation. And as it goes with speculation, they can sometimes grow pretty wild. And some of the unique traits and characteristics of the Maine Coon cat have given rise to some fantastic speculation indeed. The cat's tufted ears and feet, for instance, are similar enough to a bobcat's that it is sometimes said that the Maine Coon cat originated from a mating of a domestic cat and the wild bobcat. Another implausible theory is that the Maine Coon descended from the mating of some domestic cats and raccoons - largely because of their bushy ringed tail and their common brown tabby coloring. Both of these theories are highly unlikely. Though it is interesting to note that the name of the Maine Coon was derived from their resemblance to the raccoon, while those not of the brown tabby coat were simply called "Maine Shags."

What seems more probable is that the Maine Coon simply resulted from years of crossbreeding and natural selection. Maine is borded by the Atlantic Ocean to the East, and has had a long history of active seaports and port trade. The state is, in fact, known for its shipbuilding industry. Plenty of ships from foreign lands had landed on its shores throughout the years, thus bringing us to the other posible breed origin of the Maine Coone cat: crossbreeding with long-haired cats that arrived in Maine from the ships.

There are several versions. Some contend that the short-haired domestic breeds paired with the Norwegian Forest Cat from the Scandinavian forests that came with the Norsemen during the 11th-century, as the Norwegian Forest Cat bears striking similarity to the Maine Coone Cat in its long fur, bushy tail, sturdy body, and its large size. Others speak of a Captain Charles Coon, an English sea captain who kept an army of long-haired cats on his ship - Persians and Angoras among them. He sailed up and down the New England coast, and where he docked, so did the cats. In fact, when the local short-haired cats began producing long-haired kittens, people would usually refer to them as "one of Coon's cats."

One of the more fanciful tales involves the tragic Marie Antoinette, Queen of France. It is said that during the French Revolution, Marie Antoinette sought to escape France with the help of one Captain Samuel Clough. She had already loaded her most prized possessions on the ship, including six of her beloved Turkish Angora cats. Marie Antoinette was caught, of course, and later executed in 1793. But Captain Clough and her cats reached Wiscasset, Maine, and later bred with the domestic short-haired breeds.

Some crossbreeding does seem to figure into the Maine Coone Cat's origins, though it was more likely due to successive breeding and crossbreeding of local short-haired cats with some of the long-haired cats that were brought by settlers and seafarers who came to America. This happened naturally, and natural selection in the harsh New England winters did the rest.

The Maine Coon Cat is intelligent, loyal, and a good worker, so they became beloved pets and valued workers in the homes of the settlers. Their owners were so attached and proud of their Coon cats that in the 1860s, they began having their own cat show at the Skowhegan Fair, and Maine Coon cats all over the area vied for the title of "Maine State

Champion Coon Cat." This was followed by successive cat shows which figured the Maine Coon cat prominently.

There was a lull in the Maine Coon's popularity sometime in the 1900s when the more showy Persians grew became popular. It wasn't until the 1950s that the Maine Coon cat again caught the public's interest, and since then, with the active commitment of enthusiastic and dedicated breeders, planned breeding and pedigree registries helped establish the Maine Coon cat's modern breed standard.

In 1985, the Maine Coon cat was recognized as the official state cat of Maine.

Chapter Two: Things to Know Before Getting a Maine Coon Cat

After a brief overview of the typical traits of the Maine Coon Cat, the theories of its origins, and a brief history of its stint as a show cat, we now turn to some of the more practical aspects of cat ownership: their temperament, whether you need a license, the costs of purchasing and keeping a Maine Coon, and the pros and cons of this breed.

This will enable you to judge whether your lifestyle and home is a fit for this breed, and whether you should be looking further into purchasing one of your own.

Do You Need a License?

While there are no federal requirements in the United States for licensing cat owners, local states may have specific regulations governing pet ownership. This varies depending on your area or region, so it is always best to check with your local municipality regarding the pertinent laws in force in your state.

A cat licensing program is usually geared towards curbing cat overpopulation, and you will find that a license for neutered cats is cheaper than that for cats who are intact. These licenses are usually required to be renewed annually.

Even if your state does not require you to get a license for your cat, it is still a good idea to have them microchipped. This is actually a good idea for cats - even if they are properly licensed. The reason is that a license tag is usually attached to a collar, and sometimes those collars come off. Microchipping/ tattoing and registering ensures that you can still be identified as the registered owner even without the cat's license tags.

Be aware that in states which require cat licenses, the laws also apply to indoor cats, even if they are already microchipped. Failure to license a cat can result in a fine. Every cat of a certain age, whether kept indoors or allowed outdoors, is required to be licensed and registered in certain states. You'll never know when this comes in handy as there are various circumstances - whether foreseen or unforeseen - which can cause a separation between a cat and its owner.

Do Maine Coon Cats Get Along with Other Pets?

Maine Coon cats are a gentle and affectionate bunch, and they get along well with children and other household pets. But be advised that Maine Coons were bred to be mousers - their original work. You'll never have to fear having a mouse wandering in your home if you have a Maine Coon! That said, while Maine Coons generally get along well with other pets such as dogs and other cats, you might want to exercise due caution if you also have smaller pets such as birds, mice, or hamsters. There have been reports of Maine Coons coexisting nicely with smaller animals, but you will never truly remove their instinctive predator instinct. Caution and proper supervision is always advised.

How Many Maine Coon Cats Should You Keep?

It is up to you, as the prospective cat owner, how many Maine Coon cats you wish to keep. If you have the space for them, are able to afford their upkeep, and are willing to put in the energy and care that is required in keeping more than one cat, then by all means do so!

There are, however, some additional considerations for you to keep in mind as you consider bringing in more than one Maine Coon into your home:

- There might be some dominance displays between or among your cats, so you will likely have to provide multiple pet beds, food and water bowls, and even litter boxes. Yes, some cats dislike having to go in a box where other cats have already done their business. Allowing each cat their own space and things will reduce much of the resulting confusion and chaos that can ensue.
- Be particularly wary of bringing together a male and female cat. Unless you are planning to breed - and have the knowledge and resources to do so - then please do the responsible thing and neuter your cats. Things might get particularly rowdy when your female cat reaches her age of first heat. Having a

bunch of tom cats hanging around outside your house
might be bad enough, and mating displays between
your male and female cat might, at the very least,
become embarrassing. But having your female cat
birthing one litter after another will likely not become
more endearing with the next unexpected and
unplanned litter!

How Much Does it Cost to Keep a Maine Coon Cat?

It is very easy to underestimate the cost and upkeep
of keeping a Maine Coon - many people tend not to look
beyond the initial purchase price, and generally have a
vague idea of what pet food might cost. Before you even
think of getting a Maine Coon - you have to understand that
they will require some recurring expenses that can quickly
add up unless you have budgeted properly.

Expect to shell out more during your first year of pet
ownership, as you will be purchasing the kitten as well as
most of the tools, equipment and pet accessories you will be
needing during your first year. Add the expenses of
neutering or spaying, and the initial costs, including their
purchase price, can vary. Getting a cat from a shelter will
cost a lot less than purchasing a kitten from a reputable

breeder with all the required papers and a proud pedigree. As a general range, however, you can probably expect to shell out some $400-1,000 (£308.88-772.2) for a purebred Maine Coon. Additional initial costs include:

- Pet equipment and accessories such as a bed, collar, food and water bowls, grooming accessories, and a good range of cat toys. A good estimate for this is about $250 (£193.05)
- The costs of microchipping your cat can range from around $20-25 (£15.44-19.31).
- Spaying or Neutering, with Veterinarian fees can average anywhere from $130-170 (£100.39-131.27)
- Your cat may come to you already having received their initial vaccinations. Some additional vaccinations might be required, however, and it is a good idea to budged around $50 (£38.61) for this.

These initial costs would be in addition to the annual costs of food, cat litter, regular de-worming, flea treatments, veterinarian fees, pet insurance (when applicable), and grooming expenses. An estimated breakdown of these annual expenses are as follows:

- Food: $250-310 (£193.05-239.38)
- Cat Litter: $75-150 (£57.92-115.83)
- Worming: $50-75 (£38.61-57.92)
- Flea Treatment: $75 (£57.92)

- Veterinarian fees: $50-65 (£38.61-50.19)
- Insurance: $95-235 (£73.36-181.47)
- Grooming and other miscellaneous expenses: $250-645 (£193.05-498.07)

Keep in mind that these are just wide-margin estimates, and the moneywise cat owner can certainly find ways and means of saving. Costs may also vary depending on your location, your selection of pet products, and the rates of veterinary servies in your area. But some experts agree that a cat owner should have an emergency pet fund of at least $1,000 set aside for unforeseen emergencies - which will likely be medical in nature, just in case.

A breakdown of these expenses are shown in the table below:

Item	Initial Costs	Annual Costs
Initial Purchase Price	$400-1,000 (£308.88-772.2)	
Pet Equipment and Accessories	$250 (£193.05)	
Microchipping	$20-25 (£15.44-19.31)	
Food		$250-310 (£193.05-239.38)
Cat Litter		$75-150 (£57.92-

		115.83)
Veterinarian Fees, Spaying or Neutering	$130-170 (£100.39-131.27)	
Vaccinations	$50 (£38.61)	
Worming		$50-75 (£38.61-57.92)
Flea Treatment		$75 (£57.92)
Veterinarian Fees		$50-65 (£38.61-50.19)
Insurance		$95-235 (£73.36-181.47)
Grooming and other miscellaneous expenses		$250-645 (£193.05-498.07)

*Costs may vary depending on location
**U.K. prices based on an estimated exchange of $1 = £0.77

What are the Pros and Cons of Maine Coon Cats?

To summarize, below is a list of the pros and cons of keeping a Maine Coon cat. If you are still undecided about whether or not this is the right breed for you, read on. A

Maine Coon cat is like any other cat, but certainly bigger in so many ways. Some of these traits might be good for some, and some of their quirks might need some level of tolerance for some pet owners. The following lists should serve as a general guide on your decision as to whether the Maine Coon is the right cat breed for you:

Pros of the Maine Coon Cat Breed

- Loyal
- Laid-back and low maintenance
- Clownish and playful
- Generally healthy with few breed-specific health conditions
- Depending on your preference and living space, these are big sized cats - desirable for some, though maybe not for others
- Intelligent and trainable
- A beautiful breed, but low maintenance in terms of coat grooming
- A distinctive trill or chirp that can be delightful to hear

Cons of the Maine Coon Cat Breed

- With that abundance of long hair, they do require regular grooming. Otherwise, they can shed a lot, and their hair can get matted or tangled

- The grooming requirements may require the additional bath as some of their poop may get on the abundance of hair on their furry tails and rear ends
- Their large size does require sufficient space - especially enough running room for when they are feeling playful. If you have a very small apartment or living space, your cat might not be able to thrive as it cannot exercise or run around properly

Chapter Three: Purchasing Your Maine Coon Cat

After seeing an overview of the practical aspects of what it means to add a Maine Coon cat to your household, and your heart is still set on getting one for a pet, the next thing to do is to set out finding the right cat for you. There are many options available to prospective pet owners:

rescuing cats from a shelter should definitely be an option as you will literally be rescuing cats in need of a good home. Alternatively, you can look into getting one from a reputable breeder. If you do this right, you will be assured that you are getting a healthy cat from a good pedigree, who has undergone the proper health and medical checks. Towards the end of the chapter, we will look into the more practical aspects of preparing your home for the arrival of your new family member.

Where Can You Buy Maine Coon Cats?

The combination of cats' natural fecundity, their sheer numbers, and their tendency to wander has resulted in the unfortunate situation prevalent today of lots of homeless and semi-feral cats and kittens wandering around the world over. Many owners end up adopting stray kittens only later to learn that these are actually Maine Coons, or at least have some Maine Coon blood in their pedigree.

If you wish to help alleviate this state of affairs, you might want to consider opening up your home to one of these lost cats. There are many rescues the world over for both dogs and cats, many of them breed-specific. You can search online for one nearest you, or you can use the following list as a starting point in locating the nearest Maine Coon rescue in your area:

Maine Coon Adoptions. <http://mainecoonadoptions.com/>

Only Maine Coons Rescue. <http://www.omcrescue.org/>

Maine Coon Rescue Alliance.
<http://www.mainecoonsavers.com/>

Maine Coon Rescue. <http://www.mainecoonrescue.net/>

East Coast Maine Coon Rescue.
<http://www.eastcoastmainecoonrescue.org/ >

As an alternative, you can check out the websites of some international or internatial cat organizations that recognize the Maine Coon as a breed. They usually carry a list of cat shelters in various areas or regions, and they also carry a list of reputable breeders who have undergone intensive screening to meet with the association's standards. Check out the following links either to find a rescue or a listed breeder:

Cat Fanciers Association: CFA Breeder Assistance & Breed Rescue, Inc. <http://cfabreedersassist-rescue.org/>

The International Cat Association (TICA).

<http://www.tica.org/find-a-breeder>

The Governing Council of the Cat Fancy (GCCF): Rescue & Rehoming, Cat Welfare Rescue Directory.

<http://www.gccfcats.org/Welfare/Rescue-Re-homing>

The GCCF Breeder Scheme.

<http://www.gccfcats.org/About-GCCF/Breeder-Scheme>

How to Choose a Reputable Maine Coon Cat Breeder

If you choose to purchase your cat from a breeder, it pays to know how to choose a reputable breeder. This is important becaus there are far too many breeders out there who are only in it for the money, not the cat's best interests. On the negative side, you might end up with a maladjusted or poorly socialized cat, whose parents have not been screened for the genetic illnesses to which Maine Coons are prone to. For the good money you are shelling out to these breeders, you should at least expect some sort of assurance that the risks of any illnesses or diseases have been kept to a minimum.

So how do you go about choosing a reputable breeder? A good first step is to look at the listings of breeders among the various cat organizations that recognize the Maine Coon as a breed, such as the TICA, the CFA, or the MBCFA. You can look for these listings online, or alternatively, you can attend one of the cat shows being held by these groups. Many of those showing their cats are breeders, so right during the show you can already determine for yourself how much care and attention they give to their Maine Coons. It is probably a safe bet that such enthusiasm for the breed extends to their breeding programs.

In addition, breeders are not listed by these organizations randomly. Their catteries usually go through regular screening, and they will not be listed unless they meet the organization's standards.

Begin reaching out, either introducing yourself in person during the show, or contacting them online. You must first start a conversation regarding Maine Coons, and this is the perfect chance for you to ask questions about the breed, just to make doubly sure that this breed really is the right cat for you. A reputable breeder will usually be just as enthusiastic in discussing many of the Maine Coon's characteristics, needs, and quirks.

You can then ask to visit their cattery, which any good breeder will only be too happy to show you. You can then judge for yourself how clean the queen and the kittens are, whether they are well-fed and healthy, and how their surroundings are maintained. Ask about their feeding, health and early socialization. But be prepared to answer questions yourself. Any responsible breeder is just as interested in placing their kittens with responsible owners as you are in getting a good and healthy kitten. With proper communication, you might find yourself building a good relationship with a person who is a good source to ask about any questions you might have about your cat in the future.

When you are satisfied, you are probably going to put down a deposit for your future Maine Coon. Do this, and settle in to wait.

As a final note, it is best to avoid purchasing your cats from your local pet stores. The truth is that no reputable breeder will even consider placing their kittens in those little cages, to be displayed at the shop windows. No matter how cute they may look from across the glass windows, you simply cannot be sure about the cat's or the kitten's background and breeding history. Better to adopt from a rescue, than paying for, and inadvertently supporting, disreputable breeders who mass produce litters and sell to stores.

Tips for Selecting a Healthy Maine Coon Kitten

Once you have selected a good and reputable Maine Coon breeder, half of the job is already done. You can at least rest assured that the entire litter has been prepared for in the same way: health checks and screenings for both the stud and the queen, and a nurturing and healthy environment where the kittens were bed, born, and grew up in.

Now all that is left is to pick your kitten. Rest assured by this point that whichever kitten you pick, you are getting one that is as healthy as all the others. Perhaps the only real difference now is in the traits and characteristics that are unique for each cat.

Remember that a kitten should not be completely separated from its mother until it is at least 10 weeks of age. Some breeders wait until the kittens are at least 12 weeks before handing them over to the new owners. By this time, they should be fully weaned and are capable of living apart from their mother.

The kitten should be well-socialized, which means that it is naturally playful and curious, even with you, a stranger - though perhaps you can make allowance for some timidity and cautiousness at first. Watch out for possible signs of sickness, such as diarrhea, a stuffy nose, sticky eyes, or unnatural thinness. A kitten should be healthy, with clear eyes and nose, the beginnings of a luxurious coat, and suitably plump and cute. This means that they have a healthy appetite, are well-socialized, and will be happy to explore the rest of the world with you!

Preparing Your Home

It is generally a good idea to confine your kitten to one room in the beginning - a place where everything he needs is within easy reach: his bed, his litter, his water and food bowls, and enough toys at his disposal. Eventually, however, you can reasonably expect that they will have access to your entire home. Their natural curiosity almost demands a complete inspection of their new house. So it is always a good idea to prepare your home beforehand, to kitten-proof it (which is not unlike baby-proofing your home) so that the kitten's natural curiosity will not lead them to dangerous antics or explorations.

There can be as many dangers inside the home, as there are outside. Here are some tips for kitten-proofing your home:

- Put away any loose strings of any kind. Ribbons, dental floss, yarn - kittens love to play with them, which means they might eventually swallow them. This is potentially hazardous to your kitten, so keep those lovely bits of string secure in a high place.
- Secure or tuck away electrical cords, curtains, and cords. A loose electrical cord can electrocute your

kitten, and other loose cords can strangle them even as they play. On the other hand, you might have kittens climbing up floor-length curtains to get to the top. It's probably a good idea to flip those curtains over the rods - at least for the first few months.

- Beware that kittens also do love to nibble: so keep away plants, medication, garbage, cleaning supplies, and even your food.

- Secure water containers with tight lids to prevent accidental drowning - Maine Coons are noted for loving water, but this is potentially dangerous for kittens that venture into deep containers of water. For that matter, it's probably a good idea to put the toilet seat down.

- Secure the screens on your door and windows. Yes, cats and kittens can be escape artists, and unless you are watching them 24-7, an open door can prove to be too much of a curiosity. Don't allow those little kittens outdoors unsupervised - remember that the world is pretty dangerous for tiny kittens, and you don't want to run the risk of having them be run over by a car, climbing a tree they can't get out of, of sometimes even being kidnapped! Take all necessary precautious as you would with a child - which, essentially, your kittens are.

- Those little kittens certainly have the capacity of getting into tight spots you couldn't have imagined.

So it's always a good idea to check your appliances before turning them on: such as the washing machine and dryer. Sometimes they can hide or curl up beneath a recliner or a sofa. You are probably going to have to watch your step for the first few months as the kittens explore their new home and are liable to get underfood much of the time!

Chapter Four: Caring for Your New Maine Coon

Often nicknamed the "gentle giant," Maine Coons are good pets for first time cat owners. They are an adaptable breed, gentle, kind, affectionate, loyal, and in terms of needs and attention, he isn't high maintenance. They have a comical side to them that they retain even into adulthood. And it won't really take much effort to keep them happy. They are good-natured cats, happy to receive attention when you give it, is patient with his owners and the rest of his family, and tolerant even of the more attention-seeking pets you may have.

Maine Coon cat owners are always delighted to do what they can to keep their cat healthy - that is because they demand so little. In this chapter, you can learn more about some of the things that this breed will appreciate in his new home - from enough running space, sufficient playtime, and the occasional venture out of doors.

Habitat and Exercise Requirements for Maine Coon Cats

Because the Maine Coon is a large cat, this breed does need some exercise. Even if it is kept mainly as an indoors cat, they will still need some form of exercise through which they can burn their energy and thus keep from becoming overweight. If you have a yard, be sure to provide sufficient fencing or outdoor cat enclosures, especially if your Maine Coon is still a kitten. Whether or not you keep your cat as an indoor or outdoor cat is an owner's choice, but be sure you make this decision with the best interests of your cat in mind. Are your streets safe? Many kittens are prone to vehicular accidents, and of course, the more expensive breeds can simply be stolen. All things considered, experts are in agreement that cats do not really need to be outside.

In this day and age, doing so might actually shorten their lifespan considerably.

That said, many owners have been able to successfully keep a Maine Coon as a purely indoor cat. Occasionally, you might want to bring him outside for a walk on a harness and leash, and done often enough, this can provide your cat with enough physical and mental stimulation to keep them happy and healthy.

Don't forget to make your home conducive for your new pet, as well. As they mature, they will take up a lot of space - and you need to give them a special place in your home which they can call your own. Maine Coons are not lap cats - their size will make this quite awkward. But they do like to stay close to their owners. Their expressions of loyalty and devotion are, in fact, not unlike that manifested by dogs. They will wait at the door for when you arrive, and should you be sitting at your desk working, there's nothing they like better than curling up beside your feet to keep you company. Nothing makes them happier than to have you reach over occasionally to give them an occasional pat or stroke.

As an alternative to letting cats outside, you can probably provide them with enough space in the home that is theirs completely. Equip this space with a good cat bed, enough toys to keep them occupied, a scratching post, high resting places, and enough nooks and crannies where they can play hide. Needless to say, clean food and water bowls, and a clean litter completes their necessary environment.

The rest of it is really up to you and how you interact with your Maine Coon on a day-to-day basis. They might not demand attention, but they do require regular displays of affection and attention. And keep their bowls, litter and bed clean. As noted in a later chapter, socialization is a continuous process, and it keeps your cat from being alienated and unhappy. At the extreme, an unhappy cat may eventually grow feral if kept in an inappropriate and unfulfilling environment. Or they may simply lose their affection for you if you don't show them enough attention and affection.

Toys and Accessories for Maine Coon Cats

For a large and dignified breed, the Maine Coon is oddly clownish and a bit of a goofball, even until they mature. But this just makes them more endearing to most pet owners.

It bears remembering, however, that like most cats, Maine Coons love to play. While you might eventually gather a good selection of toys during the cat's lifetime, he might show marked preference for some toys over others, then changes his preferences over time. Each cat is unique in this, so it is as well to provide them with a good selection of toys and accessories to keep them happy.

Many times, cats will find enough play in the most random things. But it is always a good idea to provide them with toys that are theirs alone, as it would also be an expression of how special they are to you. Below are some ideas for cat toys and other cat accessories you can experiment with to see which would engage your Maine Coon's interests and attention:

- perches
- scratching posts
- a variety of toys such as ping pong balls, cardboard boxes, toy mice, bird feather teaser, catnip, laser, or anything other simple thing the can play with.

Chapter Five: Meeting Your Maine Coon Cat's Nutritional Needs

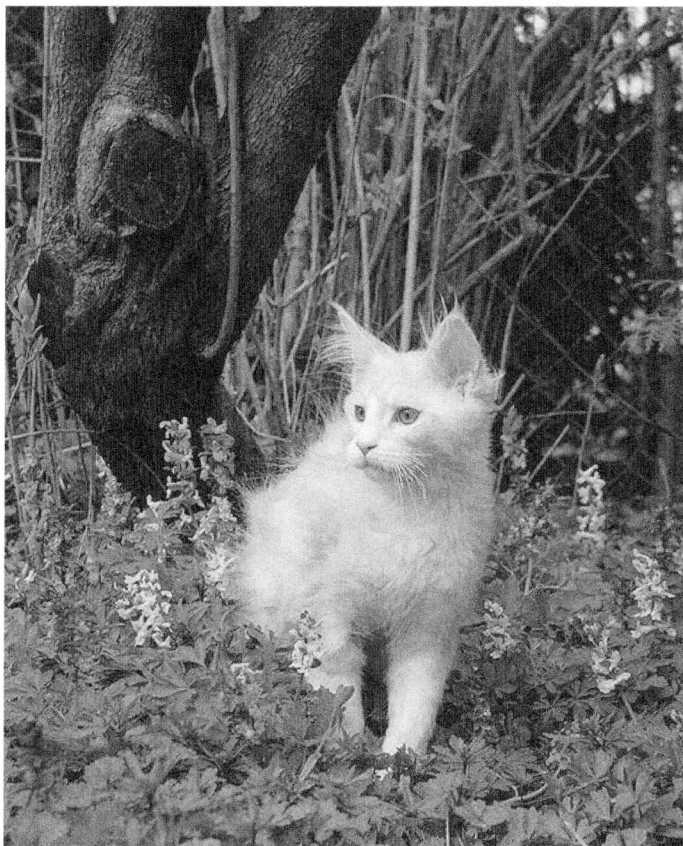

Any good and responsible cat ow ner wants to give
their Maine Coon the best, and that includes food! These
days, however, the choices are so unlimited and varying,
with widely diverging expert opinions, that it can get
confusing.

While not endorsing any specific brand or feeding program, this chapter aims to encapsulate some of the basic principles on the do's and don't's of feeding your cat. The process of finding the right cat food will likely be a journey for you as the owner, since even these guidelines will have to be adjusted to your own pet's preferences and reactions to their food, which means that you will still need to adjust accordingly. The best feedback you can get for what food and feeding regimen works best for your Maine Coon comes your cat himself. Does he eat heartily or does his appetite seem low? Does he have enough energy each day? Is he gaining too much weight? Does he seem lethargic and low on energy?

Try not to make any drastic changes in your cat's diet. If you do want to transition to something else, make the change gradually to get his stomach used to the idea of the new food. This way, you can also monitor any changes that might show with the new diet.

The Nutritional Needs of Cats

We'll try to make this section as painless as possible. Below is a breakdown of some guidelines regarding cat nutrition:

- Cats are obligate carnivores. This means that meat needs to be the main component of their diet. It shouldn't be too difficult to comprehend: remember that cats chase mice? In a natural setting, cats will gravitate towards raw meat whenever possible, and they have evolved as predators of smaller prey. Some owners swear by a raw meat diet, with additional natural supplements for nutrients that they cannot get from meat, such as vitamins A, B, C, D, and E, and calcium. Others look for high quality meat-based cat food, with the main component being either chicken, chicken meal, or fish meal.

- Avoid chicken by-products and chicken by-product meal. Mainly, these are composed of the rendered parts of the chicken, such as the head, feet, viscera, necks, undeveloped eggs, and intestines. While cats are natural carnivores, not even a cat in the wild can survive on by-products alone. They will need good, quality meat, and they will not be able to get enough nutritional value from these meat by-products alone.

- Avoid corn meal, corn gluten meal, and wheat gluten. These are cheap fillers, and are also highly allergenic, which can cause a cat to develop Irritable Bowel Syndrome or even induce vomiting. In any form, these ingredients are difficult for a cat to digest, so steer clear!

- Good grains for a cat include rice, rice flour, barley, barley flour, or milled barley. Higher quality cat food typically includes these ingredients as a good source of carbohydrates. Make sure that these are secondary ingredients in any cat food, however. Protein from meats should still be the main ingredient.
- Your Maine Coon cat should always have a readily available source of clean drinking water which he can reach at any hour of the day.
- Be on the lookout for these additional nutrients on the label, which are also necessary for your cat's daily diet: calcium, phosporous, vitamin c, and taurine

How to Select a High-Quality Cat Food Brand

You are probably going to rotate your cat food choices over time, not only to ensure that a cat gets the best possible nutrition from both canned and dry food, while also keeping a variety of food choices available for your cat so that he doesn't get bored. Rotating food choices, and in fact mixing canned and dry food is recommended by many nutritionists to give your cat a more balanced diet.

But how do you choose among the varied options of cat food currently available? First of all, do your homework. While we cannot provide specific feedback on the different brands that are commercially available, there are many helpful forums and product reviews online of cat lovers and their feedback regarding certain cat food products. Asking questions and networking among the different cat owners you meet at cat shows, at the vet, your breeder, or friends who are also cat owners, can give you very real feedback regarding actual effects or quality of specific cat food brands. Keep an open mind, but be discerning. Read, and keep abreast of new developments in the industry. There are always new products coming on the market, so part of the journey is staying informed.

In addition, you are going to have to learn how to read the label of the selection of cat food available to you. First of all, look for one that meets or exceeds AAFCO standards. And don't forget to check the expiration date on the box.

Secondly, look for age-appropriate cat food. Depending on which stage of life your cat is in, different formulations of cat food are specifically targeted to meet the nutritional needs of your cat at a specific age. Hence, choose between kitten, adult, or senior cat food.

And as noted above, look for meat-based cat food as much as possible. You can tell the primary components of any cat food by which ingredients are listed first - and these should include the following:

- Protein from meat sources such as fish, poultry, or beef
- Taurine
- Vitamins, minerals, enzymes, fatty acids
- Water

Avoid fillers such as corn, wheat, cornmeal, by products, added sugars, and artificial or chemical preservatives such as BHA, BHT, ethoxyquin, and propyl gallate.

Tips for Feeding Your Maine Coon Cat

Feeding Maine Coons are not noticeably different from feeding most other cats. Your cat's unique quirks will determine, to a large extent, the type of feeding method you will use. Some cats are finicky eaters, and the free feeding method should work well with this type of cat. Basically, you leave them food in the bowl which they can return to any time during they day when they feel hungry. This is actually recommended for kittens who will likely space out their feeding in small portions throughout the day. But this also limits your options when it comes to the type of food you give them - dry food is best since wet food, or even raw meat, will not keep if left out for too long in the open air.

And yet this is probably the best and only option for people whose lifestyles keep them out of the house more often than not. Free feeding at least ensures that your cat does not go hungry during the day when you are away. But what to do when you have a cat who is dangerously close to obesity?

You might want to consider having someone feed your cat for you throughout the day. Alternatively, there are mechanical food bowls that can be set to feed small portions at specific times throughout a day.

Another feeding method - which has been openly acknowledged as the healthier option - is scheduled feedings with controlled portions. Scheduled feeding time also allows your cat to learn some discipline, especially if you choose to take away their food bowls after their schedule is up. This teaches them that in order to feed well, they have to eat all the contents of their bowl - thus ensuring that they are getting their proper nutrition, while also keeping their food and their food bowls clean and fresh, as opposed to food that is left out in the open for too long. Others, however, choose to measure out the food portions and leave it for the cat to eat at his own pace. This might be the more feasible option for you if you have an extremely finicky cat that prefers to eat sparingly, no matter if you take their bowls away after some time.

Always remember to provide them with clean and fresh drinking water that they can easily get to throughout the day. Clean their food and water bowls daily, and don't disturb them when they are eating. Again, be attentive to your cat and his state of health, adjusting your choice of food, his daily portions, and his unique feeding preferences.

Dangerous Foods to Avoid

Not all people foods are safe for your cats to eat. Fact is, some of them can be downright dangerous! Below is a list of some of dangerous foods you should avoid giving your cat. Should your Maine Coon ingest any of the following, call the Pet Poison Control hotline right away at (888) 426 – 4435.

- Alcohol
- Apple seeds
- Avocado
- Candy and gum
- Cherry pits
- Chives
- Chocolate
- Caffeine
- Fat trimmings and bones
- Garlic
- Grapes/raisins
- Hops
- Macadamia nuts
- Milk and other dairy products
- Mold
- Mushrooms
- Mustard seeds
- Onions/leeks
- Peach pits
- Potato leaves/stems
- Raw eggs
- Rhubarb leaves

- Tea
- Tomato leaves/stems
- Tuna

- Walnuts
- Xylitol
- Yeast dough

Chapter Six: Training Your Maine Coon Cat

Cats have good memories, and the Maine Coon cat, in particular, is an intelligent breed that can certainly be taught a trick or two! Maine Coons are sometimes called the dogs of the cat world, and these gentle giants are not too dignified for learned behavior. Of course, in training a Maine Coon cat, you must start with the basics such as socialization and litter training. Once you've got these down pat, you can begin expanding your repertoire and adding tricks up their furry sleeves!

Socializing Your New Kitten

Getting a Maine Coon kitten from a reputable breeder means that your kitten is already on the way to proper socialization skills. But if your kitten still seems a bit skittish and shy rather than the friendly and affectionate cat that Maine Coon cats are known for, then it is up to you to supplement their socialization - and this must be done as soon as possible!

The ages from before 4 to 14 weeks of age are crucial to a kitten's proper socialization. This is important because he might never outgrow the natural caution and suspiciousness that most kittens have at a very young age. If they still retain these characteristics until they grow mature, you will have a very stressed-out cat that hides at the sight and sound of every strange new thing. Another disadvantage of improper socialization is that the kitten might grow up naturally averse to you or the rest of your family, and while she is part of your household, you might never experience the kind of loving loyalty and affection which Maine Coons naturally have.

Socializing a kitten is not very complicated. Just keep in mind that you shouldn't push the kitten too much too soon - especially when he is still partly dependent on her mother and the rest of his siblings.

Start out with small doses of daily and gentle handling at about 4 weeks. Once the kitten gets used to you and to being handled by humans, you can slowly begin to start expanding his range of experiences. All these should be done in a positive atmosphere, however, since the lesson you are aiming to teach him is self-confidence in the face of new and strange experiences. For instance:

- Expose him to short bursts of gentle human handling by different people
- Begin exposing him to different sights, sounds and smells around the house
- Early grooming, which is recommended to build the habit of a cat that is used to regular grooming sessions, is also a good way to socialize your kitten and to get her used to human handling.
- Consider getting her used to the feel of a collar, and then later on, a leash. While you might not need to do this for all cats, you might find this learned behavior coming in handy later on for your Maine Coon. The Maine Coon is a large breed, and being a large breed, they can be prone to obesity. Eventually, you might find it necessary to take your cat out for a walk. Besides which, taking your little kitten out for short distance walks - even if it is only until the yard - is a good learning experience that will also expand his

range of experiences. As your cat grows, you can also begin experimenting with the use of a harness.

- You can also provide him with a range of different cat toys which you can use to play with him and build your bond

- Take him with you out of the house, whether it is only for short walks, for a car ride, or a visit to the vet. During all these experiences, you should always be present and reassuring to your cat, as they will seek some form of security from you - especially if they are only just beginning to be weaned from their mother.

Once you have begun to properly socialize your kitten, it should continue throughout the rest of the cat's life. There will always be new experiences waiting for your Maine Coon, and new avenues to explore. Proper socialization can also be the beginning of a wide variety of additional training for your Maine Coon.

Litter Training for Kittens

If all goes well during the kitten's formative years, you will likely not have to do any litter training at all. In general, the elimination habits of cats are standard: they dig, eliminate, and then cover. This is instinctive, and comes from a need to hide the smell of their waste from predators.

Part of good litter habits is also your responsibility half the time, however. Make sure that it is located in a place where there is at least a modicum of privacy and where he will not be disturbed, which is also within easy reach. And keep the litter box clean - scooping twice a day and topping it off with additional litter granules, and cleaning and scrubbing the litter box at least once a week. Many times, behavioral problems regarding cats that suddenly refuse to use their litter box can be traced to their natural fastidiousness. Much as humans are averse to using a dirty toilet, neither will your cat be all that fond of using a dirty litter box. Other possible reasons for a behavioral problem among cats who refuse to use the litter box is a box that is of the right size, the wrong depth, or multiple users (i.e., different cats using the same box). Their sudden refusal to use the litter box may sometimes be due to the strong odor of cleaning chemicals you are using. Sometimes a cat may prefer using two separate boxes - one for urinating, and another for defecating; or he may prefer a specific brand of litter. As you get to know your Maine Coon, you'll figure out the quirks of his personality, including his elimination habits, and you can adjust accordingly.

Clicker Training for Teaching Maine Coone Cats Tricks

Yes, these gentle giants are intelligent and willing enough to be taught a trick or two. Some trainers who recommend using the clicker training method have reported great success in teaching Maine Coons tricks such as shaking hands, high five's, and even fetching!

No matter which trick you decide to teach your cat first, the training basics are the same. By associating the sound of a clicker with desired behavior and a treat, your Maine Coon has the capacity to pick up a variety of tricks in no time!

Here is a basic guideline to using the clicker training method to training your Maine Coon:

- First of all, get a clicker. You can purchase this at your local pet store, or online. This is a small, handheld device that makes a clicking sound when a button is pressed.
- You can use a flashlight to indicate targeted behavior. For instance, if you want them to get on top of a chair, use the light to point out the chair to let him know what your desired behavior is.
- Finally, the last factor in this training is some pre-selected treats that you can give as rewards. Make sure this is something he likes and which he will eat quickly and easily. The focus is, after all, the training, and not the food. Eventually, you will eliminate the food altogether and use only the clicker, so you need

to be able to move easily past the treats to continuous training.

Simply put, the clicker training method integrates these three elements noted above: the light to indicate desired behavior, a clicker that should be sounded at the same time that the desired behavior is being performed, and the treat that follows afterwards.

Using the clicker simultaneously with the desired behavior helps them identify which behavior is being rewarded later on. Done consistently and over time, they will gradually associate the clicker with positive and desired behavior.

You might begin by first introducing your Maine Coon to the clicker itself so that it does not get spooked later on. Have them come near the clicker, allow them to sniff it, and as you click, give them a reward. This begins their associating the clicker with something positive. As much as possible, the clicker should only be used during training, and should always be associated with rewards. This teaches them that the clicker is a good thing. Eventually, the association is formed that the behavior you are clicking is also a good thing.

Over time, you can expand the number and variety of tricks you can teach your Maine Coon. The intelligence and natural devotion of this breed makes them easy learners.

Just make sure to keep training sessions short, and always a positive experience. This is a wonderful way to nurture the bond between you and your cat, while also giving them mental and physical stimulation at the same time.

Chapter Seven: Grooming Your Maine Coon Cat

One of the reasons for the Maine Coon's great popularity is that it is relatively low maintenance in terms of grooming. Cats are fussy and fastidious by nature, so you will not have a lot of work to do. But because the Maine Coon does have a very long and elegant coat, some regular grooming is required. At least a weekly brushing session should suffice to keep their coats free of mats. But if you are showing, then you will have to learn how to bathe your Maine Coon! But this is also true for any Maine Coon owner - while you may not have to bathe your cat regularly, sometimes you might need to, especially when the abundant fur along the tail area gets a little dirty with their poo.

Tips for Grooming Maine Coon Cats

While a weekly coat care grooming session might be sufficient, you might want to get into the habit of daily or regular brushing with a soft bristle cat brush. These come with two sides, which you can alternatively use to brush and comb. You might want to focus on the Maine Coon's tail, hind quarters, and behind the ears, and brushing these regularly can keep mats from developing in the first place.

That said, sometimes matting cannot be avoided, and to be able to help the Maine Coon maintain his beautiful coat, at least a weekly coat care grooming session is recommended to winnow out any matting or tangles that may have formed despite your best efforts. You will need the following:

- de-matting comb
- grooming rake
- metal comb
- clippers
- eye wipes
- cotton balls to clean the ears

Start out by working out any tangles or knots in the coat using a metal comb. Be sure to start near the end instead of near the skin, holding the fur near the skin to lessen painful tugging. Go slow and a little at a time, carefully separating the tangled fur. As an alternative, you can use a fine-tooth comb like a flea comb for really tight knots.

Next, you can use the grooming rake to remove any dead undercoat. Remember that the Maine Coon's coat has two layers, one of which is the fluffier and softer undercoat. If ignored, this can certainly mat. Gently running the grooming rake along the fur will enable you to remove most of the dead undercoat. You'll probably be surprised at the amount of hair you'll get! Just continue gently stripping those out - then you'll discover just why your Maine Coon does need your help in maintaining all that abundant fur!

If you do find mats that are just too far gone, trying to brush them out will only hurt your cat, and eventually they might dislike grooming sessions altogether. Using a flea comb, position this between the skin and the mat, and then snip alongside the comb near the matted fur side.

Finish it off with eye wipes to clean their eyes and nose area, or you can just use a warm, damp facecloth for the face. Finish it off with cotton balls damped with warm water to clean the inside of the ears, going slowly so as not to damage the sensitive portion of their inner ears.

Tips for Bathing Maine Coon Cats

Yes, cats do need the occasional bath. You might want to start them out while they are kittens, so that even though they will probably never get to really like a bath, they will at least be trained to tolerate it. Bathing also needs to be done in a positive atmosphere, and should your cat wish to escape, just let him. Make it as painless as possible so that he does not learn to view bath time as something to be avoided at all costs. For the more mature Maine Coons, you might want to finish trimming their claws before bathing them.

Remember that the Maine Coon's abundant fur is designed to keep them warm during winter and the rainy season, so it will not get wet easily. You might want to use water in a sufficient-sized tub, or in the kitchen sink, depending on your cat's size. Keep this at a nice temperature, and just put your cat in and get him wet. Use quality cat shampoo and start rubbing it in. Add water as needed to really get the fur wet. Try to make the shampooing as quick, efficient, and as painless as possible.

Rinse well, and be sure to get all the soap off, because he'll be washing himself afterwards, and you don't want him ingesting any soap that you might not have rinsed off. Use towels to dry him off, and he's good to go. Using a dryer is probably not a good idea since this might scare him. You might want to pick a warm or hot day to give him a bath so that he can dry himself off in the sun.

Needless to say, each cat is different and unique, and you will probably need to adjust your methods depending on his preferences. It is always a good idea to start the habit of bathing and grooming when he is still a kitten though, keeping to it regularly and consistently so that it becomes a habit that stays with him throughout his life.

Other Grooming Tasks

There are other grooming tasks in addition to regular brushing and bathing, and this includes clipping your cat's claws and brushing his teeth. This sort of rounds out the grooming tasks for a Maine Coon cat, to keep this gentle giant looking spiffy and sharp!

Brushing Your Cat's Teeth

Yes, occasionally a good session of tooth brushing is good for your Maine Coon! this helps prevent tooth decay and dental infections. Look for quality cat toothbrush and cat toothpaste, and while regular brushing is ideal, doing so about two or three times a week is a good routine.

Clipping Your Cat's Claws

Clipping your cat's claws is a more humane option to de-clawing them. While providing them with a good scratching post will keep their nails reasonably sharp and trimmed, occasionally you might want to trim them once in a while. Invest in some quality cat nail clippers. Using them should be pretty easy.

Just squeeze the paw until the claw is revealed. Press them all the way out, and clip. Be cautious when clipping so that you don't cut the quick, or the flesh beneath the nail. Clip conservatively, especially if it is your first time. Withou enough practice, claw clipping should be a quick and straightforward routine, and is actually one of the easiest parts of Maine Coon grooming.

Chapter Eight: Breeding Your Maine Coon Cat

Anyone who undertakes to breed Maine Coon cats should first be aware of the huge responsibility this entails. Yes, Maine Coons are a very lovable breed, and pedigreed Maine Coons do cost good money, so it is understandable that some people might consider it desirable to try for a litter of kittens. But a prospective breeder should know that breeding cats can consume much of their time, energy, and money, so if you are only looking to make some extra money, this may not prove to be a worthwhile venture for you.

On the other hand, you should be fully committed to promoting the best interests of the breed, which means that you have to be thorough, selective, and well-informed before you even try to breed your cats. You will be responsible for the health and wellbeing of both the queen and her kittens, up until the time when you are able to place the kittens with good homes, so this is not something for the casual or spontaneous breeder to venture into.

There are those who recommend that anybody who wants to be a breeder should always start first by showing cats. This is a good way to learn about the breed, the breed standard for Maine Coons, and to network with other cat enthusiasts and cat breeders. A good and dedicated acquaintanceship to cat showing should ground any prospective breeder with realistic expectations and actual experience in dealing with the Maine Coon cats, and what it really means to breed responsibly.

That said, when done right, breeding your Maine Coon can be a very satisfying and fulfilling experience. This chapter contains some basic information, tips and guidelines that will be useful for any prospective cat breeder. First we will begin with some basic cat breeding information, and later we will take a look at some practical tips for caring for your new kittens.

Basic Cat Breeding Information

The assumption here is that you have selected a good queen and stud for breeding, and the requisite health checks have been conducted. There should be ample space for your cattery, and you should be prepared to devote a lot of time, effort and energy into seeing that the breeding process, up to the time of pregnancy, labor and weaning the kittens - goes well. It is also a good idea to have a good savings set aside for necessary expenses such as cat food, a litter and a kitten pen, and some unforeseen costs as well - such as veterinary services just in case you run into any problems.

The Queen

A good queen should be healthy and fit, and psychologically well-adjusted for motherhood. Most recommend that a cat should not be mated before her first or second year, and during this time you should already be looking into prospective studs. Be aware that cats are quite prolific, and there could be many instances of unplanned or accidental pregnancies if the owner is not careful. Female cats can mate multiple times when they are in heat, so it is not an uncommon occurrence that a litter may have been sired by more than one father. Be watchful of your queen when she is in heat - don't allow her to escape unless you wish her to mate with many of the local toms who will surely be hanging around outside! It is probably a good rule of thumb to be particularly watchful and protective of a breeding queen. When allowed to mate naturally, it is estimated that a cat can have a full litter at least three times a year!

On the other hand, it is not recommended to let a cat "call" three times in succession without mating. Since they are induced ovulators, they will only release their mature female eggs after they are mated. If a cat is unable to mate for long, there is an increased chance that cysts might form in her ovaries. If a queen is not allowed to mate for too many cycles, the eggs will accumulate until the next estrus. This can lead to two potential problems: a cat that ends up carrying too large a litter, or older eggs being carried over from previous cycles, which can result in congenitally defective kittens.

If your cat is calling and you do not want her to mate, you should ask your veterinarian about the possible ways of managing her heat cycle and fertility. This is generally done through three ways: the use of hormones, mechanical stimulation, or with the service of a vasectomized male. Consult with your veterinarian regarding these three ways of managing a queen's fertility.

A cat can have her first heat at the age of six months, and they are seasonally polyestrous. This means that they will come into heat during certain seasons of the year - usually in the spring and sumer, though cats who are kept indoors may cycle year-round. Another interesting thing to note about the cat's heat cycle is that they are reflex or induced ovulators. This means that they need to be bred first before they will ovulate. This would explain why cats in heat will mate multiple times, and why there will still be signs of heat several days after mating. This can lead to what is known as superfecundity, or when the queen's litter has been fathered by more than one male. Sometimes, a surge of hormones early during pregnancy can result in mixed gestational stages of the kittens inside her uterus, who will then be in different stages of development.

Perhaps the first thing any potential cat breeder should learn is how to manage a breeding queen - especially during times of heat and she is calling. If you are not planning on breeding, unless you wish to end up with litters of kittens during your cat's lifetime, the responsible thing for you to do is to have your female cat spayed. Not only does this eliminate the chances of unplanned pregnancies, but doing so before she reaches her first heat cycle will reduce her risk of mammary cancer.

The Feline Heat Cycle

You will recognize when your queen is in heat. During the first two days, or proestrus, she will be "calling." Some behavioral signs of this are rubbing, excessive friendliness, yowling, rolling, and a frequent desire to escape. During this time, she will also exhibit a unique posture of standing arched with her tail straight up, with her back and rear legs stiffening whenever they are touched. She will not allow mating during this time, however, and she will usually fold her tail between her hind legs to prevent this.

The second stage, or Estrus, is when mating occurs. This can last for up to ten days, though if coitus happens earlier, it can end after about three to four days. Copulation releases a lutenizing hormone (LH) that stimulates ovulation, though the levels can vary with different queens. For some, it may take several matings before ovulation can be induced. After a successful breeding, estrus terminates and diestrus begins.

It is recommended that you leave the tom and the queen alone together for several days during the estrus stage. This will allow multiple matings, and ensures a successful pregnancy. Some breeders recommend providing the tom room to escape after breeding, because the queen can get aggressive immediately after mating. She will also groom herself frantically, and she will not allow anyone near her for about an hour afterwards. After this, she becomes receptive again, and mating can resume. Again, she may allow multiple males to mate with her, so it is a good idea to keep her relatively isolated during this time, where the selected stud is the only male with access to her.

If the breeding was not successful, the queen will enter an interfollicular stage known as interestrus. This may last for about a week, during which there is no reproductive activity. Then she enters a new cycle of proestrus and estrus. If, on the other hand, she was mated and ovulated, but did not become pregnant, she enters a stage known as metestrus that can last for some 5-7 weeks. Again, there will be no reproductive activity during this time. After this stage, she will again enter a new heat cycle of proestrus and estrus.

If the mating was successful, however, the gestation period will last for about 59-65 days, or about 9-10 weeks. If, for any reason, she loses her kittens, she will again enter the estrus stage after 2-3 weeks. If she successfully carried her litter until birth, a new heat cycle will begin again when the kittens are about 8-10 weeks old.

Pregnancy

Pregnancy can be confirmed at around 3 to 4 weeks. Her nipples will become more pink and prominent, and the telltale baby bump will start to show at around 4 weeks. Queens with small litters will take even longer to "show" than those with a larger litter. To date, this is the only safe method of recognizing feline pregnancy.

The nutritional need of your queen will increase during pregnancy, and their appetite should begin to increase at around the fifth or sixth week of pregnancy. It is recommended that you begin to increase their diet by about twenty-five percent, making sure that they have a nourishing and well-balanced diet. It is a good idea to speak with your veterinarian so that you can plan out the dietary changes that will be suitable for your cat during her pregnancy.

You should also begin preparing for her due date. You might notice her seeking out secluded areas, spending more time with you and less with others in the family, or a marked hostility towards strangers. Prepare a birthing area such as a delivery box with sufficient room, and a second box in which she could move the kittens after she has given birth. Keep this in a relatively secluded area of the home where she can have peace and quiet, and try to get her used to this area some time before her actual due date. You can also begin to put together a birthing kit in expectation of the due date, which would include items such as towels, a clean bowl, sterile gloves, blunt-end scissors, betadine, pediatric bulb syringes, a tube feeder, and dental floss or suture to tie the umbilical cords if necessary. Be sure to have the number of the nearest emergency vet clinic on hand, some pen and paper, and a clock nearby.

In general, many cats are able to give birth without much trouble, but you should always be at hand, ready to lend a hand when needed. If this is your first time to assist during cat labor, you should probably seek out a mentor to stay with you and guide you during the process. Cat labor can be a frightening and stressful experience for first-timers, so while you can read up on the subject prior to the date, a friendly and helping hand with practical experience is always good to have alongside you during this time. Being able to act efficiently when needed can mean the difference between losing or saving a kitten.

Breeding Tips and Raising Kittens

In general, queens are good mothers, and they will know instinctively how to take care of their young. Allow her to settle herself and her litter in peace and without many interruptions, and without handling them for the first 24-48 hours after birth, you are allowing the queen to bond with her newborns in a peaceful and nurturing environment.

The queen will take care of pretty much everything, from nursing them, cleaning and grooming them, and even teaching them to use the litter box. Human intervention only comes in when checking them, weighing the kittens, and gentle handling for early socialization. It is not advisable, however, to take them away from their mother for prolonged periods of time as this may stress out both the mother and the kittens.

You should expect a weight gain of at least 10 grams per day. If it does not seem like the kittens are gaining much weight at all, it probably means that the mother is not producing enough milk. It is important to give her a calcium-rich diet while she is lactating, to give her the energy and the necessary nutrients to feed her young ones. Consult with your veterinarian if she does not seem to be eating well, or if any of her milk glands appear swollen. On the other hand, if any of the kittens seem cold or does not seem to be gaining any weight, bring the kitten to the veterinarian immediately.

Weaning starts at around 4 weeks. By this time, you can start providing them with high quality kitten kibbles soaked or moistened with water or kitten formula. You can encourage them to try the food by placing some on their lips and positioning them near the bowl. For the next two weeks, allow them free choice of nursing or prepared food while handling them gently and regularly as much as possible. This will help them gain both human and cat social skills within a positive environment.

The kittens should be fully weaned at around 6 to 8 weeks. At around this time, you can begin regulating the mother's diet in order to help her milk supply to dry up. Slowly decrease her food and water portions each day, until she is back to her pre-pregnancy diet levels. If she seems to have lost weight during the pregnancy and lactation period, adjust her food intake accordingly.

Chapter Nine: Showing Your Maine Coon Cat

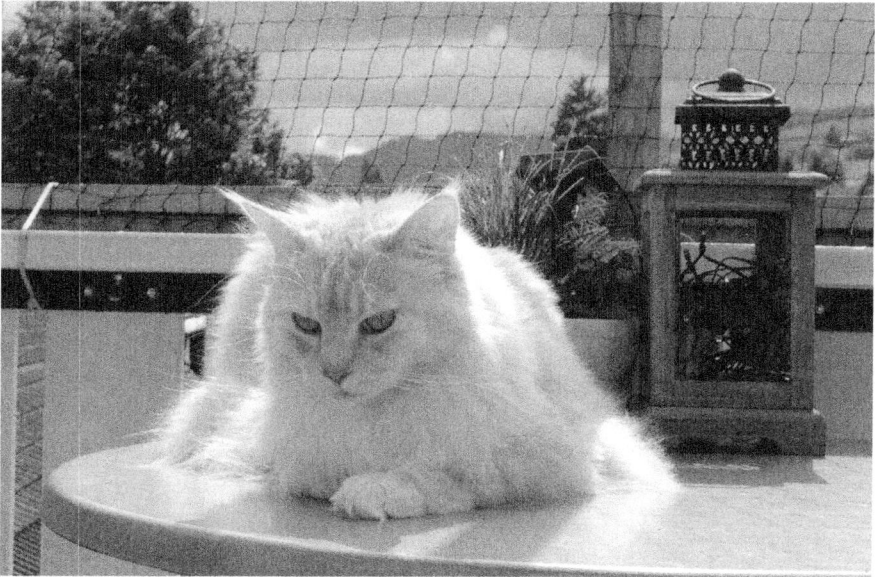

If you are considering showing your Maine Coon Cat, then it is as well to get acquainted with this breed's rich history as a show cat. This chapter will also give you an overview of the Breed Standards in several different associatons, and some practical hints and tips that will guide you as you prepare for cultivating a magnificentcat that just seems naturally meant to shine.

A Brief History of the Maine Coot Cat in Show

The Maine Coon Cat has an impressive history of being a showcat, and is, in fact, known as America's First Show Cat. As early as the 1860's, Maine farmers had their own cat show at the Skowhegan Fair, and Maine Coon Cats from all over the state where showcased, competing for the title of the "Maine State Championship Coon Cat."

One Mrs. E.R. Pierce, the owner of a Maine Coot Cat, and who documented the early history of domestic cats in the United States, particularly the Maine Coon Cat, stated that cat shows were conducted in many of the populous cities along the eastern seaboard during this decade. The largest and most famous of these shows was that held at New York's Madison Square Garden in May of 1895. The winner of this show was a brown tabby female named Cosey, a Maine Coon Cat owned by one Mrs. E.N. Barker.

Cosey was named Best in Show, and was awarded a silver medal and a silver cat collar, both marked "National Cat Show, 1895." This collar was subsequently purchased by the Cat Fancier's Association (CFA), through a generous donation from the National Capital Cat Show, and this little piece of cat history is now housed at the CFA Central Office in the Jean Baker Rose Memorial Library.

While the New York show did not take off as a yearly prestigious event, the Boston shows did. For the three years of 1897, 1898 and 1899, this was dominated by a brown tabby named King Max, owned by Mrs. Pierce.

Cat Shows eventually caught on, and spread elsewhere in the country. The Cat Fanciers Association, which was founded in 1908, kept the only breed record books at this time, and about 28 Maine Coon Cats were listed - but under a special proviso: that the owner gave a sworn statement that the sire and dam were of the same breed, long haired, and neither being short-haired.

Perhaps it was because of the lack of documented pedigree, but the Maine Coon Cats were soon overshadowed by other long-haired pedigrees, such as the Persian and the Angoras. One of the last recorded wins for a Maine Coon Cat was that of a Best in Show and First Place in his Class for a "longhaired blue Maine Cat" in Portland, Oregon in 1911. But they gradually disappeared from the show scene, and in the 1950s were believed to have become extinct altogether.

Some time in the early 1950's, cat enthusiasts Alta Smith and Ruby Dyer attempted to end this slow degeneration of the Maine Coon Cat's numbers and popularity, and they formed the Central Maine Cat Club (CMCC). They kept records of the breed and held shows and exhibitions, and for the next 11 years, they nursed the Maine Coon Cat back into popularity, including the establishment of the first written breed standard for the Maine Coon Cat.

While the CMCC soon outgrew itself, their purpose was accomplished. Maine Coon Cats began appearing in national cat shows again. And in 1968, the Universal Maine Coon Cat Club was founded, its purpose to "preserve and protect the breed."

But the Maine Coon Cat's return was not without a struggle. Thrice, the Cat Fancier's Association (CFA) denied the Maine Coon Cat provisional breed status. This led to the formation of the Maine Coon Cat Club in 1973, its members working on the requirements for the recognition of the Maine Coon Cat as a provisional breed: a standard, a breed club, and a sufficient number of registered cats.

The dedication and commitment of these early initiators were not in vain. In May of 1975, the Maine Coon Cat was given provisional status, and Championship status was given in May of 1976.

The Maine Coon Cat was back, and the years since has shown season after season of Maine Coon cats that stood out above others. To date, they are the third most popular cat breed, based on the number of kittens registered with the CFA.

Maine Coon Cat Breed Standards

The Maine Coon Cat is truly a universally popular feline, beloved by many people all over the world. In 1968, the Maine Coon Breeders and Fanciers Association (MCBFA), an international breed association for the Maine Coon Cat was founded. The breed is also recognized by a number of different cat organizations all over the world. These would include the following:

- American Cat Association (ACA)
- American Cat Fanciers Association (ACFA)
- Canadian Cat Association (CCA)
- Cat Fanciers' Association (CFA)
- Cat Fanciers' Federation (CFF)
- Fédération Internationale Féline (FIFe)
- Governing Council of the Cat Fancy (GCCF)
- The International Cat Association (TICA)

Necessarily, the Breed Standards for the Maine Coon Cat varies depending on which organization is hosting the show, so you will have to pay particular attention to the published standards, depending on which organization or association you are registered with. There are slight variations in standards, though of course the differences are not very great.

Below, and as a sort of general guideline, we will first take a look at the MCBFA's published Breed Standard, and then later take a look at some of the noticeable variations in the Breed Standards of the different organizations listed above.

1. The Maine Coon Breeders and Fancier's Association's (MCBFA) Maine Coon Cat Breed Standard

General

The Maine Coon Cat is solid and rugged, with a slow maturation. Females are somewhat smaller than the males.

Head

The head is medium in length and width, and there is a squareness to the muzzle. Some broadening is allowable in males. The cheekbones are high, the nose is medium with no break or bump. The chin is firm and in line with the upper lip and nose.

Eyes

The eyes are large, wide set, and slightly oblique. Eye color can vary from shades of green, gold or copper, though blue and odd eyes may occur in white cats. Clarity in eye color is considered desirable.

Ears

The ears are large, wide at the base, moderately pointed, and well-tufted. Lynx-like tipping is considered desirable.

Body and Neck

The body is medium to large, muscular and broad-chested. It is also long, with proportional parts, creating a rectangular appearance. There is a definite squareness to the rump, and the neck is medium in length.

Legs and Paws

The legs are wide set, substantial, and medium in length. The paws are also large, round, and well-tufted. There should be five toes in front, and four toes in back.

Tail

The tail should be long, equal in length to the body (or the distance from the end of the rump to the shoulders), wide at the base and tapering. The fur should be full, long, and flowing.

Coat and Coat Colors

The fur on the shoulders is short, though gradually increasing in length along the back and sides, ending in a long shaggy belly fur and full britches. The fur is soft, falls smoothly, and lies close to the body. There is a slight undercoat, and a frontal ruff beginning at the base of the ears.

All colors are recognized. Except for solid colored cats, white trim around the chin and lip is permitted.

Disqualifications and Penalties

The following are considered disqualifications: buttons, lockets, spots, even coat all over, a short cobby body, crossed eyes, kinked tail, incorrect number of toes. On the other hand, the following would incur penalties in scoring: untufted paws, delicate bone structure, nose break or bump, an undershot chin, and a short and rounded muzzle.

2. The International Cat Assocation (TICA) Maine Coon Cat Breed Standard

General

This is a large breed with big ears, a broad chest, substantial bone structure, and a long, hard-muscled and rectangular body, with a long, flowing tail, and tufted large feet. Overall balance and proportion are considered essential, no single feature dominating over others.

Head, Eyes, and Ears

The head is broad and shaped like a modified wedge. It should be proportional to the body, and slightly longer than it is wide. A distinct muzzle break can be seen under high and prominent cheekbones. The chin is firm, in line with the upper lip, and wide and deep to complete the square muzzle.

The eyes are large, slightly oval, with the outer corner pointing towards the base of the ear. The eyes can be of any shade of green and/or gold, though blue and odd-eyes are accepted among whites and particolors.

The ears are large, wide at the base, the outer base set just above the level of the top of the eye. The ears are set fairly high, and the inner edge of the bases of both ears not more than an ear's width apart. It is taller than its width, moderately pointed, which appears taller due to lynx tips.

Body, Legs, Feet and Tail

The bones and musculature are substantial, with a large and long torso, broad chest, and level back. The legs are medium in length, and the feet are large, round, and well-tufted.

Additional toes are allowable on the fore or hind paws, though there should only be a maximum of 7 toes on any one foot. Symmetrical expression is preferred.

The tail should be at least as long as the body, wide at the base, and tapering to the tip, with full, flowing fur.

Coat and Coat Color

The coat length is uneven, shorter on the shoulders, lengthening down the back and sides. There is a long, full, shaggy belly fur and britches. The tail fur is long, full and flowing. The frontal ruff is more developed with age.

The coat has a slight undercoat, which gives the coat some body, though the coat still falls smoothly. It should not be cottony.

For particolors, all four feet must have some white.

Temperament

The temperament must be unchallenging. Though it may exhibit fear, seek to flee, or complain loudly, it should not threaten to harm.

Allowances

Allowances are given for size differences between males and females. A tight ear set is also allowed in kittens, and a wider ear set in mature adults. Polydactyly, which may express itself in an extra dew claw or extra toes, is acceptable.

Penalties

The following traits are penalized:

- Slanted or almond-shaped eyes
- Very close ears, or those that are set straight up. Narrow bases, wide set, or flared ears are also penalized
- Weak or receding, or narrow chin
- Prominent whisker pads on the muzzle

- A Roman nose, straight, or with a pronounced bump
- Narrow torso
- Short tail
- Any of the toes or dewclaws not touching the table
- Lack of the slight undercoat or belly shag. An overall even coat is also penalized
- Obvious lockets in the coat color
- Signs of definite challenge or threat to harm in the temperament

Disqualifications

The following, on the other hand, automatically disqualify:

- A cat that bites
- Evidence of an intent to deceive
- Adult male cats without two descended testicles
- Missing tail, either in whole or in part, except as authorized
- More than five toes one each front foot, or four toes on each back foot, unless proven as a result of injury
- Crossed eyes
- Markedly smaller size, not in keeping with the breed

3. The Cat Fancier's Association's (CFA) Maine Coon Standard

General

The Maine Coon cat is solid, rugged, with a distinctive smooth, shaggy coat. It is well proportioned and balanced, with no part exaggerated. It has an essentially amiable disposition.

Head Shape, Muzzle and Chin

The head is medium in width, slightly longer in length than width, with a squareness to the muzzle. The cheekbones are high.

The muzzle is visibly square, of medium length, and blunt-ended in profile. It should not taper or appear pointed. The chin is strong, firm, and in line with the upper lip and nose.

Ears and Eyes

The ears are large, well-tufted, wide at the base, and tapers to appear pointed. They are not flared, and approximately one ear's width apart at the base.

The eyes are large, expressive, wide set and with an oval shape. Eye color can be shades of green, gold, green-gold, or copper. White cats or any cat with white may have blue or odd eyes.

Body, Neck, Legs and Feet, Tail

The body is muscular and broad-chested, of a medium to large size, and well-proportioned. The neck is mediumlong.

The legs are wide-set, substantial, medium in length, and proportional to the body. The forelegs are straight, the back legs also straight when viewed from behind. The paws are large, round, well-tufted. There are five toes in front, and four in back.

The tail is long, wide at the base, and tapering. The fur is long and flowing.

Coat and Coat Colors

The coat is heavy and shaggy, shorter on the shoulders and lnger on the stomach and britches. Frontal ruff is considered desirable. The texture should be silky, with the coat falling smoothly. Short or overall evenness of the coat is penalized.

The coat colors can be a solid color of white, black, blue, red, or cream. Tabby patterns can either be classic, mackerel, ticked. The coat can also be bi-colored, parti-colored, of a shaded or smoke color, or any other color except those showing hybridization.

It is recommended that the reader interested in registering with the CFA check the organization's published Breed Standard, which contains very specific requirements regarding coloring. This information is too lengthy to summarize or to provide in this book, but the following is a link to the CFA Breed Standard (revised as of 2016) for Maine Coon Cats:

<http://www.cfa.org/Portals/0/documents/breeds/standards/maine.pdf>

Disqualifications

The following are considered disqualifications: delicate bone structure, undershot chin, crossed eyes, kinked tail, incorrect number of toes, white buttons, white lockets, or white spots. Also a disqualification is evidence of hybridization, which may result in the colors chocolate, lavender, or the Himalayan pattern.

4. Fédération Internationale Féline (or FIFe) Main Coon Breed Standard

Membership in the FIFe spans around 39 member organizations, from thirty-seven countries in Europe, South America, and Asia, and is truly an international federation of cat registries, holding international cat shows. The following summarizes the FIFe's Breed Standard for Maine Coon cats:

General

The Maine Coon cat is large, with a square outline of the head, large ears, a broad chest, and wth a solid bone struture. The body is long, hard muscled, and rectangular, with a long, flowing tail. Good muscle tone and density gives an appearance of power and robustness.

Head

The head is medium, with a square outline, gently curved, with high and prominent cheekbones. There is a distinct transition between the muzzle and cheekbones, and the face and nose is of medium length, and there is a square outline of the muzzle. The chin is firm, in vertical alignment with the nose and upper lip.

Eyes and Ears

The eyes are large and wide-set, slightly oval but not almond-shaped. Any color is permitted, though a clear eye color is desirable.

The ears are large, wide at the base, and moderately pointed. Lynx-tufts are considered desirable, and the tufts of hair in the ears extend beyond the outer edges of the ears. The ears are set high on the head, with a very slight outward tilt, and are one ear's width apart.

Neck, Body, Legs and Tail

For males, the neck should be strong and muscled.

The body should be well-proportioned, long, with a substantial bone structure, hard-muscled, powerful, and broad-chested.

The legs are also substantial, medium in length to form a rectangle with the body. The paws are large, round, and well-tufted between the toes.

The tail should be as long as the body (from shoulderblade to the base of the tail). It is wide at the base, tapering to the tip, and with long, full, flowing hair.

Coat and Coat Color

The coat is dense, short on the head, shoulders and legs, though gradually becoming longer down the back and sides. The hind legs and belly fur are long, full and shaggy. A frill is also expected. The coat texture is silky, with distinct body, and falls smoothly. The undercoat is soft and fine, and is covered by the coarse and smooth outercoat.

All colour varieties are allowed, including all color varieties with white, except pointed patterns, chocolate, lilac, cinnamon, and fawn. Any amount of white is allowed, including a white blaze, white locket, white chest, white belly, white on the paws, etc.

Faults

The following are considered faults, and may be grounds for penalty:

- Unbalanced proportion, small size
- Round head, or a straight or convex profile
- A nose break
- Pronounced whisker pads, and a round or pointed muzzle
- Undershot chin

- Wide set and flared ears
- Slanted or almond-shaped eyes
- Fine, light bone structure
- Long or stilty legs
- Lack of belly shag, overall even coat length, and lack of any undercoat
- A short tail

5. American Cat Fancier (ACF) Association Maine Coon Standard

General

The Maine Coon cat is muscular, solid, of medium to large size, and with the look of the wild. Initially reserved towards strange people and situations, but with an amiable disposition. The females are usually smaller than the males.

Head, Ears and Eyes

The head is of medium width and slightly longer than it is wide, with an allowance for broadening and jowls among the males. The muzzle is square, the cheekbones are high, and the chin is firm and in line with the nose and upper lip. The nose is slightly concave with no break.

The ears are large, tall, wide at the base, tapering to appear pointed. They have lynx-like tips, and inner tufts that extend beyond the outer edge of the ears. The ears are set high n the head, and with a distance of an ear's width between them.

The eyes are large, round, and wide-set, with a slightly oblique setting. Clarity of eye color is desired, and may be any shade of green, gold, or amber. Solid white cats may be blue, amber, green or odd-eyed.

Body and Tail

The body is medium to large in size, muscular and broad-chested. The body is long and well-proportioned, creating a rectangular appearance. The neck is medium to long. The body is solid, with firm muscle and no flabbiness.

The legs are studily-boned, medium in length, and the feet are large, round, and well-tufted underneath and between the pads.

The tail is long, at least as long as the body, wide at the base and tapering to the tip.

Coat and Coat Color

The coat is uneven in length, and subject to seasonal variations. The fur is short on the head, neck, and shoulders, gradually becoming longer along the back, towards the tail and down the sides towards the belly. Britches and belly fur are full and shaggy. The coat flows smoothly, and texture may vary depending on the color, though not fluffy. Frontal ruff is heavier on the males than on the females. The tail is heavily furred, though not bushy.

All colors except solid colors should have white trim around the chin and lip line. As with the CFA, the ACF also provides specific guidelines regarding coat colors and coat patterns, which you can check out here:

<http://www.acfacat.com/Breed%20Standards/MAINE%20C OON.pdf>

Penalties

Poor condition such as flabbiness, obesity, dull coat, emaciation, or any evidence of illness, poor physical condition, or lack of proper grooming, are penalized. Also points to penalize are untufted paws, a Persian-like break in the nose, a Persian-like undercoat, short tail, and a short, rounded muzzle.

Disqualifications

The following are considered grounds for disqualification, or withholding:

- A delicate bone structure
- Overall even coat
- Undershot chin
- Short cobby body and legs
- Kinked tail
- Crossed eyes

- Polydactylism
- Lockets
- Groin spoits or other small white spots on full-colored coats and patterns.

6. Governing Council of the Cat Fancy (GCCF) Maine Coon Standard

General

The Maine Coon Cat is a semi-long haired cat distinguished by is large size, bone structure, rectangular appearance, and flowing coat. It is muscular, with a rugged outdoor appearance, a characteristic weatherproof coat, and the demeanor of an alert and capable hunter.

Head, Ears and Eyes

The head is medium in length, the nasal bridge equidistant from the ear line and the tip of the nose. The head is slightly longer than the width, though allowance is given for additional breadth of jowls in males.

The muzzle is square, with a firm chin, a fairly full cheek and high cheekbones. The nose is of uniform width, with no sharp break or stop.

The ears are large, tall, wide at the base, and tapering to appear pointed at the tip.

The eyes are full and round, spaced wide apart, slightly oblique in setting. They may be of shades of green, gold or copper. Odd or blue eyes are permissible in white cats.

Body and Neck

The body is of large to medium size, solid and muscular, with a broad chest. The rump is square, the body is long and rectangular in appearance together with proportionate limbs.

The neck is moderately long, and thick and muscular among mature males.

Legs, Paws and Tail

The legs are substantial, the paws are large and round. The toes are carried close, five in front, and four behind.

The tail is long, as long as the length of the back, wide at the base, and tapering towards the tip. The tail fur is long, profuse and flowing, not bushy.

Coat and Coat Colors

The coa is waterproof and virtually self-maintaining, with the undercoat being covered by a more substantial glossy top coat. The fur is shorter on the head, neck and shoulders, increasing in lenth down the back flanks, and tail. The coat should not be fluffy.

The breeches and belly fur are full and shaggy, and the frontal ruff begins at the base of the ears, which are heavier among the males.   Frontal ruff is heavier among the males, and the tail fur is long, profuse, and flowing, though not bushy. The ears are feathered and preferably tufted at the ears, while the ear feathering should extend beyond the outer edges of the ear. The paws are tufted, with long tufts under the paws that extend backwards to crate a snowshoe effect.

Coat colors come in a variety of solid colors, tortoiseshell, tabby colors of classic or mackerel patterns either with or without silver, shaded and smoke, bi-color, and parti-color.

More specific guidelines are provided as to coat colors, which you can check out through this link:

<http://www.gccfcats.org/Portals/0/MaineCoon.SOP.pdf>

Faults and Disqualifications:

The following are considered faults:

- Unsound base coats in solid or tortoiseshell colored cats
- Tabby markings in adult smoke colored cats
- Heavy tabby markings in shaded colored cats
- Tarnishing in Silver
- Heavily brindled coats in Tabbies

- White color beyond the throat in non-silver tabby cats that are registered as without white

Disqualifications or Withholding of Awards are for the following:

- Polydactylism
- Wrong registration and neuters
- Blue or odd eyes in cats of colors other than white
- Van patterned cats
- Cobby body shapes and fine bone structure
- Lack of white on all four paws, belly and chest for bi-colors and parti-colors
- Nose break or stop, or a pronounced nose bump
- Untufted paws
- White markings other than those allowable, including buttons, lockets or spots
- Overall even coat length
- Persian-like coat texture
- Pattern or color faults that are considered serious
- Chocolate, Lilac and Siamese colors

Preparing Your Maine Coon Cat for Show

If you are considering having your Maine Coon Cat follow in the footsteps of his illustrious show ancestors, you should do your homework well in advance. Showing your cat can be rewarding and fun, but it is can also be challenging, demanding, and sometimes even frustrating.

The first thing you should do is to make sure that you know what you are doing. This entails gathering sufficient information: which cat show do you plan to enter (by which organization), which category, the requirements for entry, and Breed Standard of the organization. As we have already seen in the earlier part of this chapter, the Breed Standards can vary depending on which organization is hosting the show. In addition, not all shows have the same categories open to everyone, and each category has its distinct standards - from age, to whether or not they are pedigreed, registered, altered or unaltered, and whether or not they are declawed. Take note that the CFA often does not allow declawing.

Most shows usually allow for four categories: Kittens, Championship, Premiership, and Household Pet (HHP). The latter, or HHP, is a good place to begin if you are just starting out in the show circuit, as it is usually less stressful and demanding, and they are more relaxed than the other categories which typically focus on pedigreed cats and written standards. The HHP category, on the other hand, focuses more on beauty, health and temperament, and allows altered and mixed-breeds of known or unknown heritage.

Perhaps one of the best things you can do is to go to a show or several shows and observe. How do these shows proceed? Who are the judges? How are the cats handled, and how are they judged? Talk to the other cat enthusiasts there, whether pet owners or breeders, and don't hesitate to ask questions. Not only will you find other people with the same interests, you will also learn a lot - including what it is like to introduce your Maine Coon into cat shows, the costs, the preparations you need to undertake, the pros and cons, and how you can join.

Next, secure a copy of the organization's rules and regulations, a listing of their shows, their list of requirements, and their Breed Standard. Go through the Breed Standard and the organization's rules carefully. It will save you a lot of time and trouble later on if you catch any potential disqualifications right at the outset. Maybe your perfectly beautiful and standout Maine Coon cat didn't win simply because he doesn't meet a technical requirement - not because he isn't the best cat there. Knowing what you are getting into might save you some frustration and even heartbreak later on.

Then spend the next few weeks or months preparing your beloved cat. Bring him to the Vet for a thorough exam, and make sure his vaccinations are up to date. Keep him healthy, well-groomed, and most of all, try to get him used to being confident and adaptable even in changing circumstances. They will be handled and surrounded by strangers during the show, and personality traits such as shyness, timidity, or even hostility to strange people, strange cats, and new surroundings will not endear them to the judges. Try to see how adaptable they are to being handled by unfamiliar people, and give them some experience in crowded places. They may simply need some time to adapt or adjust. A show cat, as they say, is one that simply enjoys being shown.

A Maine Coon can be a perfect breed for just this - they are quiet, calm, confident and well-mannered cats. But of course not all cats are the same. If you have a somewhat more frisky, excitable, or retiring cat, they might adapt with more experience. But if they don't, entering them into a show might be more stress than is good for them.

If your Maine Coon has just the right temperament for a show cat, try to get your own feet wet by attending as many cat shows as you can - just to get your own bearings. Bring your Maine Coon along with you on some of these shows, just to see how he behaves in such an environment. Clarify any confusion or vagueness you might have regarding the rules, the Breed Standard, or the organization's requirements. Then, when both you and your Maine Coon are psyched up and ready - go ahead and sign up!

Here are a few reminders when entering a cat show:

- Make sure you have filled up the required forms completely and with the correct information or detail. Once you are listed, double-check all the information again. If you find any inconsistencies, wrong numbers or spelling, have them corrected immediately.
- Pay the required fees. Some shows also offer "special requests" for additional fees, such as extra cage space and extra grooming space. If these are things you will need, put in the request early.
- If the show is being held out of town, make the appropriate reservations for your lodgings or accommodations, and give plenty of allowance for your travel time. Needless to say, make sure you have budgeted properly for these events, as the costs will add up.
- Groom your cat well. By this time, you should have a good grooming routine, and how long it takes. Some like to bathe their cat a few days before the show itself, some during the day before, and still others a few hours right before the show. There are no hard or fast rules regarding this, so it is really up to your preference as the owner, and how best to show your Maine Coon to great advantage!

Below is a final checklist of things to remember as you prepare for the upcoming show:

- Make sure that all your papers and documents are in order, packed, and ready to hand. Include your confirmation letter, proof of vaccinations, and the show's rules and regulations.
- Bring enough money to cover fees, expenses for transport, food, supplies, and accommodations. Give yourself some leeway for unexpected expenses.
- Bring your grooming supplies along with you, just in case. You may not have enough time for a full grooming, but you might want to give your Maine Coon a few touchups right before the show. Don't forget to include nail clippers.
- Bring the necessary supplies: water and food for your pet as well as for yourself, water and food bowls, a cage, cage curtains, a pet or bed for inside the cage, his beloved pet toys to keep him entertained while waiting, a litter pan and cat litter (if not provided), and a trash bag for cleaning up.
- Bring along some extra clothes for yourself, and make sure that your shoes are are comfortable. You might also want to bring along a small first aid kit for unexpected emergencies. Remember, you and your Maine Coon are surrounded by other cats!
- Needless to say, don't forget to bring your cat!

You will probably need to stay at the show for the entire day, or until the show is finished. Some don't allow the entrants to leave while the show is still in progress - even if you have already finished your turn. If you are done, relax, have a look at the other cats or what exhibits or shows are available.

The most important thing is that you should enjoy yourself. A cat show is an experience all its own, and while it can sometimes be stressful, it can also be fun and a definite learning experience!

Chapter Ten: Keeping Your Maine Coon Cat Healthy

Maine Coon Cats are generally healthy, hardy and robust. The breed has adapted itself to the harsh New England climate, and they are good hunters, so this breed is a survivor. That said, there are some health concerns that are of particular concern in Maine Coons. While most responsible breeders do their best to screen out potential diseases by breeding only healthy cats, there is never any guarantee that a cat will not get some disease during his lifetime. The best thing that you, as the owner, can do, is to be aware of which particular health conditions Maine Coon cats are prone to, what the symptoms are, and the treatment options. Virtually any disease that is caught and treated early is less worrisome than one that has gone undetected for a long time.

Common Health Problems Affecting Maine Coon Cats

Some of the common conditions that may affect Maine Coon Cats include:

- Feline Hypertrophic Cardiomyopathy (HCM)
- Spinal Muscular Atrophy (SMA)
- Hip Dysplasia (HD)
- Polycystic Kidney Disease (PKD)

Feline Hypertrophic Cardiomyopathy

Feline Hypertrophic Cardiomyopathy (HCM) is the most common heart disease in cats, and it is potentially fatal. It is the number one cause of spontaneous death among indoor adult cats. This is a genetic or inherited condition, and is estimated to show up in 1 out of 3 among the Maine Coon cat population.

In HCM, there is a thickening in the heart's left chamber, which restricts blood flow and causes the heart to overwork. This used to be a genuine problem to screen out because most of the time, the first and only symptom among cats is sudden death to HCM. And because it doesn't manifest until a cat is a young adult or older, breeding out this condition was not easy. By the time it manifests, a cat may already have sired several litters - general good health notwithstanding.

The good news is that the genetic carrier for this disease has already been identified. A Dr. Kathryn Meurs has isolated the genetic mutation which causes HCM this disease. DNA-based screening is now available to identify cats that are carriers, and this will be signicant in the breeding of cats, thus reducing the risk of this genetic condition being passed on to new generations.

But this is a relatively recent development, and given that this is a congenital condition that does seem to occur among Maine Coons, knowing when to recognize the symptoms is always a good idea.

HCM is not an easy condition to detect outside of DNA screening - but if you find your cat manifesting respiratory difficulties, sudden hind leg paralysis due to clotting, loss of appetite, lethargy, coughing, severe weight loss, a weak pulse, abnormal heart murmurs, a bluish discoloration in the footpads and nailbeds, or a sudden collapse, you had better bring your Maine Coon to a vet. After ruling out other possible causes such as hyperthyroidism, hypertension, and cardiac arrythmias,

HCM can be diagnosed through a non-invasive ultrasound called an echocardiogram, supported by x-rays, an EKG, and an electrocardiogram.

There is currently no cure for HCM. The treatment options for Maine Coons diagnosed with HCM are mostly medications that aim to relieve the symptoms - such as by controlling heart rate, alleviating pulmonary congestion, and reducing the likelihood of thromboembolism. When feasible, a catheter can be used to remove the pleural fluid to help the cat breathe more easily.

The prognosis is variable - HCM is a progressive disease,which means that it will grow worse over time, though the rate of progression is also variable. Depending on the cat's response to medication and treatment, some can still have an excellent quality of life for several years.

Spinal Muscular Atrophy (SMA)

SMA is a non-fatal, genetic condition that is well-documented among Maine Coons. In SMA, the neurons in the spinal cord that activate skeletal muscles in the trunk and limbs are compromised, which leads to muscle weakness and degeneration. Possible syptoms include a swaying rear end, abnormal posture, difficulty in jumping, or an awkward landing when they jump down. If you feel at their hind legs, you may be able to recognize reduced muscle mass.

Symptoms can manifest as early as 3-4 months, and while not fatal, SMA can cause weakened muscle development. SMA does not affect the cat's appetite or their capacity in excretion. Thankfully, neither are the symptoms fatal, and aside from weakened muscles, a cat can otherwise live a normal life. To date, the oldest diagnosed cats are in their 8-9 years of age. On the other hand, however, some cats diagnosed with SMA may end up with paralysis in the hind legs.

A DNA test is available to diagnose and/or screen carriers of this genetic condition. Take note that this is an autosomal recessive trait, which means that two copies of the gene, or both parents who are carriers, are required for their offpsring to develop SMA. There is no treatment for SMA, but some cats do seem to stabilize and may still live comfortably for many years.

Hip Dysplasia

Hip Dysplasia is an inherited trait that Maine Coons are prone to. In the same way that this is more prevalent among the larger breed of dogs, hip dysplasia is also more common among large breed cats. A genetic predisposition for this condition is inherited, but the condition itself develops over time. There is a laxity in the hip joints which can be destabilized by having to bear abnormal weight. When this happens, the cartilage can disintegrage, resulting in arthritis and pain. As the cartilage disintegrates, the femoral head and acetabulum rub together with each step, and this may lead to osteoarthritis.

The symptoms depend on the severity, and while some cats may experience little or no pain, it may eventually cause severe lameness in others. If untreated, hip dysplasia can be crippling.

Some of the symptoms to watch out for are slow movement in the cat, a stiffness in walking, lameness, or a reluctance in running or jumping. If caught early, the condition can be managed, and some experts recommend weight management, massage, and exercise therapy. It is imperative that the cat should not be exposed to cold weather, since this might induce arthritis. Alternatively, medication or surgery can help relieve the pain for the more advanced cases.

This is another condition that can be tested for, and any cat breeder is responsible for having the hips of their Maine Coon breeding pair x-rayed and graded. This can be done when the cat is about two years of age, and a good breeder must have a result that is either fair, good, or excellent.

Polycystic Kidney Disease (PKD)

PKD is another inherited disorder; it is a slow and progressive disease affecting the kidneys. A kitten will usually be born with cysts, or fluid-filled cavities, in the kidneys. These will grow larger as the cat matures, and it is estimated that there could be anywhere from 20 to 200 cysts present.

The symptoms can manifest early, though sometimes not until 3 to 10 years of age. The initial signs are usually quite ambiguous - such as lack of appetite, depression, drinking and urinating more often, a less shiny coat. As the condition progresses, the symptoms can also be more severe, including blood in the urine, bad breath, vomiting, and weight loss. Eventually, this might lead to incurable kidney failure. It bears stressing, however, that the symptoms are very variable, and some cats with PKD may not display any of the symptoms at all - though these are usually those with very little or small cysts.

As with most inherited conditions, the best way is to remove cats diagnosed with PKD from breeding programs. This minimizes the risk of transmission to offspring. A DNA test is available to screen for the responsible gene, but at present, this test is only available for Persians and Exotics. Diagnosis is usually done by ultrasound. Maine Coons that have been diagnosed with PKD should not be bred, and cats that are intended for breeding should be tested at a year old, and retested again at the age of 2.

While there is no cure, treatment options are geared towards managing the symptoms. In cases of dehydration or vomiting, for instance, intravenous feeding for several days, followed by a special diet, is prescribed. Alternatively, therapy, a special low protein diet, and medication may be recommended to help alleviate some of the symptoms.

Preventing Illness with Vaccinations

Over the years, vaccines have been developed against potentially lethal diseases. Essentially, vaccines contain a minute, weakened or killed dose of the disease itself, in order to stimulate the production of antibodies within the cat's system. The memory of these antibodies are retained, and anytime there is re-exposure to the same pathogen, the body immediately produces more of the same antibodies. That is why vaccines are named for the diseases that they target - and in this way, immunity is built up within the cat's body against many of the lethal feline diseases.

Some vaccines are necessary and legally required - these are considered "core" vaccines, and are obligatory. The core vaccines include those for feline rhinotrcheitis, calicivirus, paleukepenia, and rabies. Rabies vaccines are required to be renewed once every one to three years, depending on your local laws.

On the other hand, "non-core" vaccines, while not mandatory, are administered depending on whether it is needed. Your veterinarian can give you the best advice on whether any of the following vaccines are needed, depending on the state of feline health in your area or region: Pneumonitis, FeLV or Feline Leukemia, FIV

or more commonly known as Feline AIDS, FIP or Feline Infectious Peritonitis, Chlamydia felis, Bordetella, and Giardia. If your Vet recommends any of these non-core vaccines, be sure to discuss with him the reason why they are needed.

Proper information and informed decisions about the administration of non-core vaccines are becoming a source of debate in the veterinary world. It seems that too much vaccinations may actually have the opposite effect of giving your pet immunity against certain diseases. The administration of a second dose of the same vaccine, when the antibodies produced with the first vaccine are still in the bloodstream, might just end up deactivating those antibodies, thus exposing your pet to unnecessary risk. That aside from certain adverse reactions that a cat may have from being vaccinated too often. Then again, others argue that any adverse reactions are rare, and that it is still safer for your pet to receive the recommended vaccines, including the annual booster shots.

Regardless of which side of the debate you come down on, however, it is important that your cat be in good health at the time of vaccination. You will be introducing foreign agents in your cat's system, and he needs to be in good condition in order to produce the necessary antibodies. If you suspect that your cat is having an adverse reaction to a vaccine, bring him to a Vet immediately.

Below is a sample schedule of feline vaccinations, though please remember that each cat's vaccine schedule will have to depend on different and variable factors such as age, environment, lifestyle, and the cat's medical history.

Below is a general vaccination schedule for kittens to give you a general idea of how vaccinations will be administered. Please keep in mind that this is only a general guideline, and your own cat's schedule may vary depending on the recommendation of your Vet:

Age	Core Vaccines
6-8 weeks	FVRCP Vaccine (Feline Viral Rhinotracheitis Calicivirus and Panleukopenia)

	Also recommended to start Heartworm Prevention
9-12 weeks	FVRCP Booster FELV Vaccine (Feline Leukemia Virus)
16 weeks	FVRCP Booster FELV Booster Rabies Vaccine

** Keep in mind that vaccine requirements may vary from one region to another. Only your vet will be able to tell you which vaccines are most important for the region where you live.

Maine Coon Cat Care Sheet

With time, your familiarity with the nuances of caring for your Maine Coon, as well as your bond with your beloved cat, will grow. Occasionally, you may wish to reference certain information or details without having to go back through this entire book. This section is intended to help you by summarizing some of the key points you will need to know about your Maine Coon: from general information, health and grooming concerns, or in matters of breeding. Always remember, though, that the process of being a responsible cat owner is a lifetime journey of learning and growing. Use this book as a starting point, or to further your knowledge - but you will probably soon discover that the responsibilities of cat ownership entails a continuous learning process.

1.) Basic Maine Coon Cat Information

Pedigree: unknown

Breed Size: medium to large

Weight: average 8 to 18 lbs (3.6 to 8.2 kg.)

Body Type: large body, robust bone structure, well-muscled

Coat Length: uneven coat length; shrt on the head and shoulders, gradually increasing in length along the back and sides, ending in full britches, long, shaggy belly fur, and full, long and flowing fur along the tail.

Coat Texture: soft but with body, falling smoothly and lies close to the body

Color: wide variety of colors with patterns ranging from solid, parti-colors, bi-colors, tabbies, shaded, and ticked

Eyes: eyes are large, with a slight oblique setting

Ears: large, wide at the base, moderately pointed and well-tufted

Tail: long, wide at the base and tapering, with full, long and flowing fur

Temperament: friendly, affectionate, loving, loyal and goofy

Strangers: cautious with strangers, though never mean or shy

Children: kind, playful, and very good with children

Other Pets: gets along with dogs and most other pets

Exercise Needs: provide adequate exercise and mental stimulation, such as perches, adequate running room, and sufficient playtime

Health Conditions: generally healthy but prone to some hereditary conditions such as Feline Hypertrophic Cardiomyopathy (HCM), Spinal Muscular Atrophy (SMA), Hip Dysplasia (HD), and Polycystic Kidney Disease (PKD)

Lifespan: average 9 to 13 years

2.) Nutritional Needs

Nutritional Needs: water, protein, carbohydrate, fats, vitamins, minerals

Calorie Needs: varies by age, weight, and activity level

Amount to Feed (kitten): feed freely but consult recommendations on the package

Amount to Feed (adult): consult recommendations on the package; calculated by weight

Feeding Frequency: four to five small meals daily

Important Ingredients: fresh animal protein (chicken, beef, lamb, turkey, eggs), animal fats, digestible carbohydrates (rice, oats, sweet potato)

Important Minerals: calcium, copper, iodine, manganese, magnesium, potassium, selenium, zinc, and phosphorus

Important Vitamins: Vitamin A, Vitamin C, Vitamin B, Vitamin D, Vitamin E, Vitamin K

Look For: AAFCO statement of nutritional adequacy; protein at top of ingredients list; no artificial flavors, dyes, preservatives

3.) Breeding Information

Sexual Maturity (female): average 5 to 6 months

Sexual Maturity (male): 8 to 9 months

Breeding Age (female): 12 months, ideally 18 to 24 months

Breeding Age (male): at least 18 months

Breeding Type: seasonally polyestrous, multiple cycles per year

Ovulation: induced ovulation, stimulated by breeding

Litter Size: about 4 kittens

Pregnancy: average 63 days

Kitten Birth Weight: 90 to 100 grams (0.198416 to 0.22 lbs.)

Characteristics at Birth: eyes and ears closed, little to no fur, completely dependent on mother

Eyes/Ears Open: 8 to 12 days

Teeth Grow In: around 3 to 4 weeks

Begin Weaning: around 4 to 6 weeks, kittens are fully weaned by 8 weeks

Socialization: between 8 and 13 weeks, ready to be separated by 14 weeks

Index

D

Q

R

S

T

U

Photo References

Page 1 Photo by bella67 via Pixabay.
<https://pixabay.com/en/cat-animal-pet-maine-coon-694718/>

Page 11 Photo by karla31 via Pixabay.
<https://pixabay.com/en/maine-coon-cat-pet-relax-camacho-216394/>

Page 19 Photo by Harald Wehner via Wikimedia Commons.
<https://commons.wikimedia.org/wiki/File:Cat-MaineCoon-Lara1.png>

Page 29 Photo by Takashi Hososhima via Wikimedia Commons, as uploaded by Dodo bird.
<https://commons.wikimedia.org/wiki/File:Karin_Maine_Coon.jpg>

Page 39 Photo by Mueller-rech.muenchen via Wikimedia Commons.
<https://commons.wikimedia.org/wiki/File:Maine_Coon_female.jpg>

Page 45 Photo by Mueller-rech.muenchen via Wikimedia Commons.
<https://commons.wikimedia.org/wiki/File:Maine_Coon_Kitten.JPG>

Page 55 Photo by Krh315 via Wikimedia Commons. <https://commons.wikimedia.org/wiki/File:Bluesmoke_Maine_Coon_Female_cat.jpg>

Page 63 Photo by ristivojevic via Pixabay. <https://pixabay.com/en/cat-maine-coon-animal-coon-kitten-1215358/>

Page 69 Photo by CStern via Pixabay. <https://pixabay.com/en/cat-maine-coon-long-haired-cat-pet-1089609/>

Page 81 Photo by LSC via Pixabay. <https://pixabay.com/en/cat-lamp-cat-face-animals-113607/>

Page 111 Photo by lakki290268 via Pixabay. <https://pixabay.com/en/maine-coon-cat-teeth-674080/>

Page 123 Photo based on derivative work by David Shankbone via Wikimedia Commons. <https://commons.wikimedia.org/wiki/File:Maine_Coon_cat_by_Tomitheos.JPG> based on original image by Tomitheos. <https://commons.wikimedia.org/wiki/File:Maine_Coon.JPG>; derivative work by David Shankbone via Wikimedia Commons. <https://commons.wikimedia.org/wiki/File:Maine_Coon_cat_by_Tomitheos.JPG>

References

"About Coonskin Cat Maine Coons." Coons'Kin Maine Coon Cats. <http://www.coonskincats.com/about_us>

"America's First Show Cat - The Maine Coon Cat." The Cat Fancier's Association. <http://cfa.org/Breeds/BreedsKthruR/MaineCoon/MCArticle.aspx>

"Breed Standards." MCBFA. <http://www.mcbfa.org/breedinfo.html>

"Breeding And Caring For Your Pregnant Cat." Dr. Hines. <http://www.2ndchance.info/pregnantcatcare.htm>

"Breeding Cats." CatsInfo.com. <http://www.catsinfo.com/breeding.html>

"Caring for Kittens Until They Are Weaned." PetWave. <http://www.petwave.com/Cats/Basics/Breeding/Weaning.aspx>

"Cat Breeding." peteducation.com. <http://www.peteducation.com/article.cfm?c=1+2139&aid=891>

"Cat Food Ingredients: The Good, The Bad, And The Ugly!" Maine Coon Cat Nation. <http://www.maine-coon-cat-nation.com/cat-food-ingredients.html>

"Cat Labor - Should You Interfere?" BreedingCats.com.
    <http://www.breeding-cats.com/cat-labor.html>

"Cat Licenses." Winnipeg.
    <http://www.winnipeg.ca/cms/animal/licenses/cat_licensi
    ng.stm#5>

"Cat-Proof Your Home in 12 Easy Steps." The Humane
    Society of the United States.
    <http://www.humanesociety.org/animals/cats/tips/cat_pr
    oofing_your_house.html>

"Cat Showing FAQ Part I: Deciding to Show." Barbara
    French, Tarantara Cattery.
    <http://www.fanciers.com/other-faqs/show-faq-pt1.html>

"Cats - Should You Let Them Out?" The Cat's Whiskers.
    <https://thecatswhiskers.wordpress.com/2006/08/12/cats-
    indoors-only-or-with-access-to-outdoors/>

"Choosing The Best Cat Food." Maine Coon Cat Nation.
    <http://www.maine-coon-cat-nation.com/best-cat-
    food.html>

"Choosing the Best Feeding Method for Your Cat." petMD.
    <http://www.petmd.com/cat/nutrition/evr_ct_best_feedin
    g_method#>

"Do Maine Coons Need a Special Diet?" MaineCoon.org.
    <http://mainecoon.org/do-maine-coons-need-a-special-
    diet/>

"Do Maine Coon Cats Need Special Care?" MaineCoon.org.
    <http://mainecoon.org/do-maine-coon-cats-need-special-
    care/>

"Feline Estrous Cycle." BreedingCats.com.
    <http://www.breeding-cats.com/estrous-cycle.html>

"Feline Pregnancy." BreedingCats.com.
    <http://www.breeding-cats.com/felinepregnancy.html>

"Food: Diet and Nutrition." Susan Dorey Designs.
    <http://www.susandoreydesigns.com/cats/food.html>

"Foods Your Cat Should Never Eat." WebMD.
    <http://pets.webmd.com/cats/ss/slideshow-foods-your-
    cat-should-never-eat>

"Grooming Your Maine Coon Cat." Adam McKinnon.
    <http://world-of-maine-coon-
    cats.blogspot.com/2008/05/grooming-your-maine-coon-
    cat_10.html>

"Heart Disease (Hypertrophic Cardiomypathy) in Cats."
    petMD.
    <http://www.petmd.com/cat/conditions/cardiovascular/c
    _ct_cardiomyopathy_hypertrophic#>

"Heart Disease in Cats." Dr. Karen Becker.
    <http://healthypets.mercola.com/sites/healthypets/archiv
    e/2012/05/28/feline-hcm-treatment.aspx>

"How to Bathe a Cat Without Fuss." Maine Coon Cat Nation. <http://www.maine-coon-cat-nation.com/bathe-a-cat.html>

"How to Choose an Experienced Cat Breeder." petMD. <http://www.petmd.com/cat/care/evr_ct_cat_breeders>

"How to Kitten-Proof Your Home." Dr. Marty Becker, DVM. <http://www.vetstreet.com/dr-marty-becker/how-to-kitten-proof-your-home>

"Hypertrophic Cardiomyopathy (HCM). Cornell University Hospital for Animals. <http://vet.cornell.edu/hospital/Services/Companion/Cardiology/conditions/HCM.cfm>

"Introduction to Queen Care." BreedingCats.com. <http://www.breeding-cats.com/queen.html>

"Is Toilet Training Your Cat a Good Idea?" Pam Johnson-Bennett. <http://www.catbehaviorassociates.com/toilet-training/>

"Keeping Your Indoor Cat Happy." Anita Kelsey. <http://www.cfba.co.uk/keeping-your-indoor-cat-happy.html>

"Letting Cats Outisde, is It Okay?" Maine Coon Cat Nation. <http://www.maine-coon-cat-nation.com/cats-outside.html>

"Maine." Wikipedia. <https://en.wikipedia.org/wiki/Maine>

"Maine Coon." cattime.com. <http://cattime.com/cat-breeds/maine-coon-cats>

"Maine Coon." FIFe. <http://www1.fifeweb.org/dnld/std/MCO.pdf>

"Maine Coon." Vetstreet. <http://www.vetstreet.com/cats/maine-coon#history>

"Maine Coon." Wikipedia. <https://en.wikipedia.org/wiki/Maine_Coon>

"Maine Coon At a Glance." hillspet.com. <http://www.hillspet.com/en/us/cat-breeds/maine-coon>

"Maine Coon Breed Group (MC/MCP).TICA. <http://tica.org/pdf/publications/standards/mc.pdf>

"Maine Coon Cat." ACF. <http://www.acfacat.com/Breed%20Standards/MAINE%20COON.pdf>

"Maine Coon Cat." CFA. <http://www.cfa.org/Portals/0/documents/breeds/standards/maine.pdf>

"Maine Coon Cat Breed Profile." Your Cat. <http://www.yourcat.co.uk/Cat-Breed-Profiles/maine-coon-cat-breed-profile.html>

"Maine Coon Cat Grooming Tips." Maine Coon Cat Nation. <http://www.maine-coon-cat-nation.com/cat-grooming-tips.html>

"Maine Coon Cat Health Problems." Maine Coon Cat Nation. <http://www.maine-coon-cat-nation.com/maine-coon-cat-health-problems.html>

"Maine Coon Cats: Health Problems Owners Must Know About." pethelpful. <https://pethelpful.com/cats/Maine-Coon-Cats-Health-Problems>

"Maine Coon Cat Training." Sandy Robins. <http://www.catchannel.com/about-maine-coons/maine-coon-training.aspx>

"Maine Coone General Type Breed Standard." GCCF. <http://www.gccfcats.org/Portals/0/MaineCoon.SOP.pdf>

"Maine Coon Grooming Tips." MaineCoon.org. <http://mainecoon.org/maine-coon-grooming-tips/>

"Maine Coon Kitten Health." Elaine Wexier-Mitchell, DVM. <http://www.catchannel.com/about-maine-coons/maine-coon-kittens.aspx>

"Managing Fertility of Your Queen." BreedingCats.com. <http://www.breeding-cats.com/managing-fertility.html>

"MCBFA Health Information & References." MCBFA. <http://www.mcbfa.org/healthfiles.html>

"Meet the Maine Coon." Pamela Merritt. <http://www.wayofcats.com/blog/meet-the-maine-coon/1897>

"Nutrition." Feline Nutrition Foundation. <http://feline-nutrition.org/nutrition>

"Our Recommended Vaccination Schedule for Dogs, Cats, Puppies and Kittens." vetco. <https://www.vetcoclinics.com/resource-center/dog-vaccinations/>

"Polycystic Kidney Disease (PKD) in Persians and other Breeds." Dr. Ingrid Putcuyps. <https://pawpeds.com/pawacademy/health/pkd/>

"Queening Supplies." BreedingCats.com. <http://www.breeding-cats.com/queening-supplies.html>

"Showing Cats." CatsInfo.com. <http://www.catsinfo.com/showing.html>

"Showing FAQ Part II: What To Do at a Cat Show." Barbara French, Tarantara Cattery. <http://www.fanciers.com/other-faqs/show-faq-pt2.html>

"Socializing Your Kitten." cattime.com. <http://cattime.com/cat-facts/kittens/82-kitten-socialization>

"So You Want To Start Breeding." The Maine Coon Cat Club. <http://www.maine-coon-cat-club.com/breed/breeding/index.html>

"Spinal Muscular Atrophy." International Cat Care. <http://icatcare.org/advice/cat-health/spinal-muscular-atrophy>

"Spinal Muscular Atrophy." Langford Veterinary Services. <http://www.langfordvets.co.uk/diagnostic-laboratories/diagnostic-laboratories/general-info-breeders/list-genetic-tests/spinal>

"Spinal Muscular Atrophy in Cats." Vetinfo. <https://www.vetinfo.com/spinal-muscular-atrophy-cats.html>

"Spinal Muscular Atrophy (Maine Coon). Dr. Laurent Garosi, Dr. Simon Platt. <https://www.vetstream.com/felis/Content/Disease/dis06227>

"The Annual Cost of Pet Ownership: Can You Afford a Furry Friend?" David Weliver. <http://www.moneyunder30.com/the-true-cost-of-pet-ownership>

"The Costs of Keeping a Cat." Pet Web Site. <http://www.petwebsite.co.uk/cats/buying-a-cat/the-cost-of-keeping-a-cat>

"The Maine Coon: America's Native Longhair." Mike and Trish Simpson. <http://www.unm.edu/~njmoore/MainCoonHistory/History.htm>

"The Maine Coon: Cat Breed FAQ." Laura Cunningham, Jean Marie Diaz, JoAnn Genovese, Valerie Johnston, Dave Libershal, Orca Starbuck, Betsy Tinney, and Eric Williams. <http://www.fanciers.com/breed-faqs/maine-coon-faq.html>

"Things to Consider Before Breeding Cats." PetWave. <http://www.petwave.com/Cats/Basics/Breeding/How-To.aspx>

"Unique Health Issues Affecting Maine Coons." MaineCoon.org. <http://mainecoon.org/unique-health-issues-affecting-maine-coons/>

"Vaccination." Jean Hofve, DVM. <http://www.moosecoonsmc.com/Vaccinations.html>

"Vaccinations." SPCA. <http://www.spca.org/page.aspx?pid=418>

"Vaccinations for Kittens and Cats." WebMD. <http://pets.webmd.com/cats/guide/cat-vaccinations>

"What Are The Best Maine Coon Grooming Tools?" MaineCoon.org. <http://mainecoon.org/what-are-the-best-maine-coon-grooming-tools/>

"What Is the Best Cat Food - and How to Choose?" petful. <http://www.petful.com/food/what-is-the-best-cat-food-how-to-choose/>

"What's a Maine Coon?" Maine Coon Adoptions.
  <http://mainecoonadoptions.com/whats-a-maine-coon/>

Feeding Baby
Cynthia Cherry
978-1941070000

Axolotl
Lolly Brown
978-0989658430

Dysautonomia, POTS
Syndrome
Frederick Earlstein
978-0989658485

Degenerative Disc
Disease Explained
Frederick Earlstein
978-0989658485

Sinusitis, Hay Fever,
Allergic Rhinitis Explained
Frederick Earlstein
978-1941070024

Wicca
Riley Star
978-1941070130

Zombie Apocalypse
Rex Cutty
978-1941070154

Capybara
Lolly Brown
978-1941070062

Eels As Pets
Lolly Brown
978-1941070167

Scabies and Lice Explained
Frederick Earlstein
978-1941070017

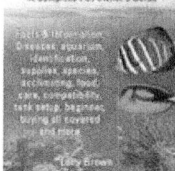

Saltwater Fish As Pets
Lolly Brown
978-0989658461

Torticollis Explained
Frederick Earlstein
978-1941070055

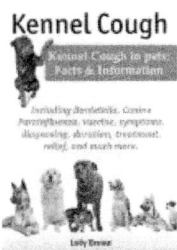

Kennel Cough
Lolly Brown
978-0989658409

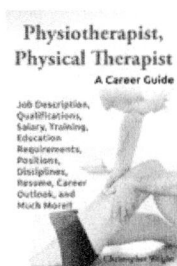

Physiotherapist, Physical
Therapist
Christopher Wright
978-0989658492

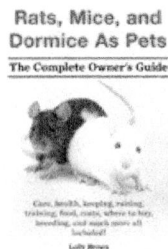

Rats, Mice, and Dormice
As Pets
Lolly Brown
978-1941070079

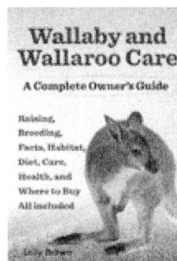

Wallaby and Wallaroo Care
Lolly Brown
978-1941070031

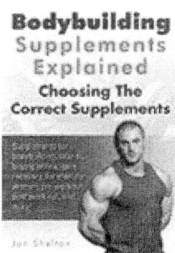

Bodybuilding Supplements
Explained
Jon Shelton
978-1941070239

Demonology
Riley Star
978-19401070314

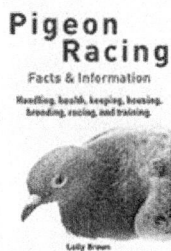

Pigeon Racing
Lolly Brown
978-1941070307

Dwarf Hamster
Lolly Brown
978-1941070390

Cryptozoology
Rex Cutty
978-1941070406

Eye Strain
Frederick Earlstein
978-1941070369

Inez The Miniature Elephant
Asher Ray
978-1941070353

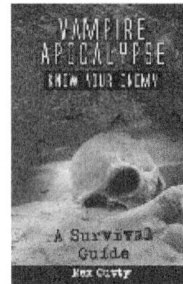

Vampire Apocalypse
Rex Cutty
978-1941070321

Printed in Great Britain
by Amazon